Best wishes,
Christmas 2020

Jeanne Wolfe

In the Hollow of God's Hand

THE
LIFE AND TIMES
OF
EDWARD Z. YODER

Joanne Wolfe

Eaglefeather PRESS

Nova Scotia, Canada

Copyright © 2018 by Joanne Wolfe

All rights reserved. No part of this book may be reproduced or transmitted in any form or by any means, electronic or mechanical, including photocopying, recording, or any information storage and retrieval system, without permission in writing from the author, except in the case of a brief quotation in critical reviews.

Published by Eaglefeather Press, Nova Scotia, Canada

Printed in the United States of America
First printing May 2018

Design: Marisa Dirks, M Design
ISBN 978-0-692-12146-7

DEDICATION

*For Jan Kreider,
without whose encouragement and support this book
would not have been written.*

*And for my mother, Charity Loretta Rebecca Yoder Laib,
who kept her father's stories alive.*

TABLE OF CONTENTS

Introduction 10
Prologue 14

PART ONE: The Lonely Years 17

1. A Better Life 18
2. Pride and Hypocrisy 23
3. Uncle John's Story 26
4. Freedom Bound 32
5. In the Hollow of God's Hand 36
6. Immigrant Train 40
7. Dakota Days 46
8. Free Land 53
9. Bemidji-Gu-Mog 56
10. The North Woods 62
11. Smallpox in Camp 72
12. The Homestead 78
13. Stopping the Silk Train 85
14. Danger in the Mines 90
15. Thieves in the Night 99
16. Threshing 102
17. New Friends 110
18. A Parting of the Ways 118
19. Courting 125
20. Oregon Bound 132

PART TWO: The Peace Church 143

21. The Bishop's Daughter 144
22. Alice's Secret 152
23. Opposition and Inner Turmoil 159
24. Love Finds a Way 165

TABLE OF CONTENTS

    25. The Wedding 170
    26. Stealing a March 177
    27. Chosen by Lot 182
    28. Birth and Death 189
    29. A Preacher's Way 194
    30. Rumors of War 201
    31. Taking a Stand 206
    32. Mennonites and War 212
    33. Lynch Mob 221
    34. "We Have a Right"..........................227
    35. Influenza and Armistice 229

PART THREE: Home 237
    36. Storyteller 238
    37. Guests at the Table 247
    38. Fire! 253
    39. The Barton Bridge Gang
         and Other Adventures.....................261
    40. On the Farm 267
    41. Starting Over — Again 275
    42. Hard Times and Farewells 281
    43. Hunger and Scarlet Fever..................289
    44. A Wedding and Two Funerals 296
    45. Back to the Homeplace....................304
    46. World at War 310
    47. Home 316

Epilogue 322
Genealogy 326
Bibliography 331
About the Author 337

LIST OF ILLUSTRATIONS

1. The author and her grandfather, Edward Z. Yoder 10
2. Headstone of Nancy Anna Zook Yoder 14
3. Young Edward with stepbrother Frank 18
4. Huge buffalo wolves roamed the prairie 26
5. Edward and his sister, Lydia, circa 1897 32
6. Edward's mother, Nancy A. Yoder, circa 1870s 36
7. Soo Line immigrant cars, Kenmare, North Dakota 40–41
8. Town square, Kenmare, North Dakota, early 1900s 40
9. Sod home on the prairie 46
10. Buffalo bones were collected and shipped East 49
11. Bemidji, Minnesota, 1896 56
12. Train depot at Bemidji, Minnesota 59
13. Lumberjacks haul white pine over ice roads 62
14. Cookee blows his horn to call 'jacks to dinner 66
15. Sky pilot Francis E. (Frank) Higgins with sled dogs 71
16. Promotional flyer for Frank Higgins talk 71
17. Edd Yoder in lumber camp, circa 1902–03 72
18. Men clear snow from a railroad cutbank 78
19. Edd Yoder's North Dakota claim shanty and granary 82
20. Kenmare Hard Coal, Brick and Tile Company 90
21. The Brickyard Mine in Tasker's Coulee 93
22. Brickworks at the Brickyard Mine 94
23. Alice Troyer's friends by the cook car, North Dakota 102
24. Edd Yoder's crew cutting grain, North Dakota 105
25. Edd Yoder threshing, North Dakota 110
26. Yoder crew harvesting grain, North Dakota 113
27. Edd's Homestead Proof, 1908 118
28. Edward Z. Yoder, 1908 132
29. Kenmare, North Dakota in winter 138–39

LIST OF ILLUSTRATIONS

30. Alice Pearl Troyer, 1908 144
31. Alice Troyer and Agnes Andrews 152
32. Alice Troyer with cousins and friends 158
33. Wedding of Edward Z. Yoder and Alice P. Troyer 170
34. Edward Z. Yoder, 1908 .... 182 and Front Cover
35. Zion Mennonite Church, early 1900s 194
36. Ezra B. Yoder with brother Dan C. Yoder 206
37. Permits for visiting conscientious objectors, WWI 212
38. The big red barn, Troyer–Yoder homestead 238
39. Madame Hendron Mama doll, circa 1925 271
40. Paul Emmons Yoder 282
41. Lois Mae Etta Yoder 283
42. Charity Loretta Rebecca Yoder 287
43. Young Kathryn with huge cabbage 291
44. Edward Z. Yoder, Jr. 294
45. Amos Peter Troyer, 1930s 296
46. Edward Z. Yoder: "Thank God for salvation" 304
47. E.Z. Yoder family, early 1940s 310
48. Edd Yoder with namesake grandson 313
49. The big red Troyer–Yoder barn with berry vines 316
50. Taking berries to the Woodburn cannery 316
51. Kathryn Grace Elnora Yoder 320
52. Alice and Edd Yoder on the Troyer–Yoder homestead 321
53. A last look at Edd's Dakota homestead ..... 322 and Back Cover

*The author, Nancy Joanne, age two,
with her grandfather, Edward Z. Yoder.
Nancy Joanne is the only grandchild named after
Edd's real mother, Nancy Anna Yoder,
who died when he was five months old. He felt
that early loss keenly, all his life.*

INTRODUCTION

MY GRANDFATHER, EDWARD Z. YODER, was a storyteller, a raconteur, and an orator. He was neither loud nor boisterous, but rather sober and soft-spoken. In his later years, he could be stern. But his storytelling was legendary. So much so that his children knew his stories by heart and passed them along to the next generation almost verbatim.

Much of this biographical account, then, is in his own words via the stories he told. In some cases, the words come from his letters and sermons. I have tried not only to be true to the content of the stories, but also to their cadence. Although I don't remember the sound of my grandfather's voice, I like to think that I know the cadence through listening to his children (my mother, aunts, and uncles) recount his stories using almost identical language and tone.

Rather than begin this biography with my grandfather's childhood, I have chosen to let him tell about that part of his life himself via his reminiscences as an adult. Stories his children and grandchildren loved — especially about his dogs, Old Rover and Silly — are told in his voice rather than in mine. Each chapter focuses on an event or series of events that my grandfather believed shaped his life in critical ways, and each reveals an aspect of his character.

IN THE HOLLOW OF GOD'S HAND

As a journalist, my job is to research the actual facts behind his stories: the times, dates, names, and places. As a storyteller, my mission is to recount the stories as my grandfather did: sparely, but with sufficient drama and emotion to engage the reader. As a grandchild fascinated by his charisma and adventurous life, my hope is to keep his stories alive to this and future generations of an increasingly dispersed clan.

To accomplish those goals, I visited the places my grandfather lived, sometimes repeatedly, and talked with the people who lived there, some of whom were alive in his time. I interviewed his children numerous times over a forty-year period and relied heavily upon such interviews, particularly those with Paul, Charity (my mother), Marjorie, and Kathryn. As the eldest daughter, my mother's memories were especially vivid and descriptive, even in the months before she passed away at age ninety-three. As family historian before me, Kathryn graciously shared a wealth of information about her father's life.

I've also spent many hours of research time in historical societies and libraries, acquired government documents pertaining to land ownership and wartime records, and read extensively on topics as diverse as nonresistance and North Dakota train schedules. Along the way I made some delightful discoveries, including photographs and information about Edd Yoder's life that are part of the larger historical record but were unknown to his family. I have remained true to the facts as I found them in letters and documents, and secondarily in the memories of his children, while attempting to spin an engaging narrative. When documents and personal memories disagreed, I kept my account true to the

INTRODUCTION

documentation. When neither documents nor reminiscences were available, I filled in the gaps with historically appropriate information and dialogue.

With a few exceptions, the names in this book are true names of actual people. In certain cases, discretion dictated using only the first initial of a last name, or simply a title followed by a dash. The names and locations of towns, buildings, streets, and landmarks are accurate to the best of my knowledge.

In writing about another person's journey, one cannot help but reflect on one's own. As the writing of this book stretched over a forty-year period, I understood my grandfather's ambitions, failures, disappointments, and successes in a more intimate way as my own life stages unfolded. That has been particularly true as I wrote the final chapters and could see larger world events that are deeply affecting me in my own time beginning to rhyme with events in his. As I sought to keep the emotional distance required to accurately tell someone else's story, I nevertheless found my grandfather's experiences and how he coped with the challenging times he lived in resonating deeply for me in the present. I hope that Edd Yoder's descendants — both direct descendants and those of his Zion church family — will find the same inspiration in his story that I have, and forgive any errors or omissions in the telling.

This, then, is the story of a life lived joyfully, sometimes painfully, and always faithfully, in the hollow of God's hand.

Joanne Wolfe
Eggleston, Virginia
April 2018

*Nancy Anna (Zook) Yoder, wife of Ezra B. Yoder and mother of Lydia and Edward Z., lies in the cemetery at South Union Mennonite Church in West Liberty, Ohio. A verse inscribed on her tombstone reads:
I'll soon be at home in Heaven / For the end of my journey / Now I see / Many dear to my heart / Are waiting and watching / Long for me.*

PROLOGUE

A BITTER DECEMBER WIND FLATTENED the thin grass and sent flurries of icy snow scudding across iron-hard ground. It shivered across the open hilltop and whipped the women's long black skirts back and forth as they hugged their heavy woolen cloaks close to their sides.

The small gathering of mourners was dressed in dark-colored clothing. The women wore unadorned, hand-sewn dresses and plain, smooth bonnets anchored by strings that tied beneath their chins. The men sported full, bushy beards and wore wide-brimmed hats and straight-cut woolen jackets that fastened with hooks and eyes instead of buttons. They were Amish–Mennonites, and they listened quietly as their minister solemnly intoned the funeral rites in German.

When the minister finished speaking, people began to move toward their wagons and buggies, stopping first to talk with a somber-faced young man who held a small girl by the hand. His other arm cradled a shawl-wrapped bundle. A young woman stepped forward and spoke softly to the man in German.

"If you are willing, Ezra, I will take the little one and care for him at my parent's home," she said, and reluctantly he handed the five-month-old baby boy to his sister-in-law, Salome Zook.

Together they walked to their plain black buggies, which soon joined a line of similar conveyances pulling out of the cemetery onto the country road. Behind them, a raw scar of frozen earth marked the newest of only twenty graves ranked along the eastern edge of the churchyard, which sloped into a snow-shrouded valley.

The year was 1881. The young man's name was Ezra B. Yoder, and he had just buried his twenty-six-year-old wife, Nancy.

The baby boy, Edward Z. Yoder, was my grandfather.

This is his story.

PART ONE

The Lonely Years

*"God hath measured the waters
in the hollow of his hand, and meted out heaven
with the span, and comprehended the dust of the earth
in a measure, and weighed the mountains in scales,
and the hills in a balance."*
— ISAIAH 40:12

Young Edward, left, *with his stepbrother Frank.*

CHAPTER 1: A Better Life

PALE SHAFTS OF MARCH SUNLIGHT struggled to pierce the cow barn's dusty windows, snagged on splintery wooden stalls, and spiraled upward on reeking gusts of ammonia that rose from a mountain of manure. Two young men stood knee-deep in the steaming pile, rhythmically wielding their shovels. The implements chuffed softly in unison as they sank into the dark mass.

"C'mon, Edd Yoder, I bet you I've put more miles on my shovel than you got on yours since breakfast time," Levi Miller joked.

"That's 'cause your shovel's half as big as mine," Edd drawled good-naturedly, flinging his shovelful onto the big wooden sledge and stooping quickly for another.

Again and again the two boys bent and scooped and flung until the heavy black muck filled the sledge, then they rested a moment while straining Percheron horses dragged the sledge through the barn's wide double doors and out to the field, and a second sledge took its place.

Around the village of West Liberty, Ohio, Amish and Mennonite farmers were taking advantage of unseasonably warm March weather to spread manure on their fields in preparation for spring planting. Seventeen-year-old Edd had hired out to the

Miller family for a week to help the Miller's three sons — Levi, John, and Samuel — load and dump manure while their father tilled it into the soil. Levi, the youngest at fifteen, had been assigned shovel duty alongside Edd.

When the morning was half spent, however, Levi called to his brother, "Say John, I'll take a turn at driving now," and John good-naturedly jumped off the sledge and took Levi's place in the stinking barn. Later, John switched with Samuel, and so it went. As a hired man, it wasn't for Edd to ask for a turn at driving, but all day he waited for one of the other boys to suggest it. By noon break, his arms and back were aching. By midafternoon, his shoulder muscles had turned into a red-hot iron bar. By quitting time, he could scarcely straighten his back and push his arms through the sleeves of his ragged jacket. As he looked up from fastening the hooks on his jacket he saw Levi nudge Samuel with his elbow and grin as he jerked his head toward Edd.

All week Edd worked in the cow barns and all week the Miller boys took turns loading and unloading, driving out into the fresh air while Edd choked on the stench in the enclosed spaces. At night he stumbled home, scraped the manure off his clothes and heavy work shoes, ate supper in a daze of exhaustion, and fell into bed. But his body ached so badly that he was scarcely able to sleep. No part of him was exempt from discomfort: standing knee-deep in manure made his legs and feet as sore as the shoveling made his arms and back, and his eyes and lungs burned from the ammonia fumes long after he left the barn.

At the end of the day on Saturday, Abe Miller handed Edd two silver dollars and a fifty-cent piece for his work. Again, Edd noticed Levi and Samuel exchange looks. This time neither boy smiled.

As he walked painfully down the road toward home that night, Edd felt very much alone. He remembered walking down this same road on his first day of school, eleven years earlier. Shortly after his mother died, Edd's father had married her sister, Lydia, and soon there were two new brothers and a baby girl in addition to Edd's older sister, also named Lydia but nicknamed Lyddy. Although Edd's clothes were always clean, they were plain and patched, his pant legs and shirtsleeves often too short for his rapidly growing body. Busy with her new babies, his stepmother left it to nine-year-old Lyddy to make sure that Edd was dressed and fed.

Edd remembered looking forward to starting first grade, but his first weeks in the high-ceilinged, one-room brick schoolhouse were anything but pleasant. He was the only new student who could not speak English. Even Samuel Miller, starting school early at five and a half, spoke enough English to get by. In Edd's German-speaking home, however, no one had taken the time to make sure he could speak and understand both languages. At recess the other children first ignored him, then taunted him, calling him "dummy" and worse. But the stocky little blond-haired, blue-eyed boy refused to cry. Instead he vowed to learn English well and, once he had, never to speak German again.

Now Edd was nearly eighteen years old, and three stepsisters and two stepbrothers still lived at home. Although sister Lyddy had married the year before and was living in Missouri, the Yoder house was still quite full. Yet, as much as he loved his younger brothers and sisters, Edd often felt as though he were outside the family circle. So when his stepbrothers, Frank and Dan, were old enough to help Pa with the farm work, Edd began hiring out as a laborer. At age fifteen he worked a grown man's day in the fields, sometimes earning only a dollar or two a week. Whenever he could, he saved those dollars for the day when he was old enough to be on his own.

Edd's thoughts circled back to his week of working at the Miller farm. Maybe the Miller boys were jealous of the money he earned doing the same job they did for nothing. That was nothing new. Often Edd was indifferently treated by the Mennonite families who hired him but resented having to do so. He, in turn, thought they were hypocrites, preaching brotherly love and fellowship at church on Sunday and then acting as though they'd never heard of such things during the week. As he gazed down the long empty road ahead of him, his square jaw clenched and his full lips tightened.

There must be a better way to live, he thought. Surely there's a happier life for me somewhere. Determinedly, he vowed to find it.

CHAPTER 2: Pride and Hypocrisy

EARLY ON SUNDAY MORNING Edd hitched the farm horses to the spring wagon and helped his mother and sisters climb over the wagon's high wooden sides. Then he and his brothers squeezed in to sit beside the girls on backless benches temporarily placed in the wagon box. His father took the reins and they began the long drive to South Union Church. The girls chattered together excitedly. Uncle John and Aunt Mattie Kauffman had arrived yesterday on the train from North Dakota to visit all the relatives and attend their daughter Fannie's wedding; they would be at church and would join the family later for Sunday dinner. Everyone was anxious to hear about the Kauffmans' adventures in wild Dakota Territory, which had only recently been admitted to the Union and divided into the states of North and South Dakota.

In church, Edd's sore muscles ached as he tried to find a comfortable position on the hard bench, but he was grateful for a day of rest. As the minister exhorted the congregation to avoid the sin of pride, Edd wondered what Uncle John would tell about homesteading on the prairie. He tried to imagine those wide-open spaces and the rolling grasslands he'd heard were so different from the flat, cultivated farmland and groves of hardwoods around West Liberty. Indians still lived in Dakota, it was said, and longhorn cattle vied with herds of antelope for a share of the rich prairie grasses. Maybe someday he'd get to see the Wild West for himself, Edd mused.

After the service, families lingered in the churchyard, enjoying the weak March sunshine and the chance to visit with seldom-seen neighbors and friends. A group of young men leaned against the porch railing talking and laughing quietly. Although he was soberly and plainly dressed, Edd's half-brother Frank had new shoes, and he turned his foot this way and that to admire the shiny black leather.

"Say Frank, are those Walk Overs?" Levi Miller asked.

"No, they're Bostonians," Frank said nonchalantly.

"Mine 'r Walk Overs; my dad says those wear the best," Levi stuck out his foot to show off the latest fashion in men's footwear.

"Oh, I don't know," John Kurtz chimed in, "I got a pair of Bostonians last month and they don't hardly pinch my feet at all."

Edd looked from John, Frank, and Levi's feet to his own, which were encased in heavy, everyday work boots. He'd cleaned the manure off them, of course, and greased them well on Saturday night, but they stuck out of his too-short pants like doorknobs stick out of a door. Edd ducked nimbly under the porch railing and sauntered toward the buggy shed. His face flushed and his ears burned as he untied the horses from the long hitching rail and began fastening their harness to the wagon traces.

I shouldn't care if Frank and Dan and the girls have nicer clothes than I do, he thought. I'm the oldest and not in school

PRIDE AND HYPOCRISY

anymore, and Ma probably thinks I don't mind anyway. But all the way home he was quiet on the wagon bench and he kept his boots tucked behind his sister Ola Mae's full skirts.

Huge buffalo wolves roamed the Dakota prairies.

CHAPTER 3: Uncle John's Story

TALK AND LAUGHTER FLEW BACK AND FORTH across the big dining room table as the Yoders and Kauffmans enjoyed a Sunday dinner of home-cured sausage, mashed potatoes, piccalilli, white and brown breads, dried-apple pie, and Edd's favorite hickory nut cake. Round and jolly, Aunt Mattie Kauffman bubbled over with delight as she visited with her younger sister, Edd's stepmother Lydia. Uncle John was quieter, but he held everyone at the table spellbound when he pushed his chair back from the table and told about Dakota.

Northwestern Dakota Territory was only beginning to be settled in 1899. Although Congress had passed the Homestead Act in 1862 and opened up frontier lands for the taking, the Civil War had slowed the westward surge of pioneers. Then, too, until recently Indians still claimed parts of the Dakotas as their own. Herding the Hidatsa, Dakota, Sioux, and Cheyenne onto reservations had not been accomplished without bloodshed. Many settlers were afraid to venture too far into territory where civilized neighbors were few, so land rushes occurred first in Iowa, Nebraska, Minnesota, and Kansas — states that were closer to the settled regions east of the Mississippi.

IN THE HOLLOW OF GOD'S HAND

Uncle John told how cattlemen drove thousands of longhorns from Montana, Saskatchewan, and Ontario to the Dakotas to fatten them on little bluestem and buffalograss on their way to the stockyards in the East and South. Those cattle ranchers fought to keep the prairie unfenced; they even made a deal with the surveyors to delay opening the area around the Des Lacs lakes for settlement for a year after it was platted, but they couldn't get around the government forever. Too many immigrants were willing to bet Uncle Sam they could live on a homestead claim and farm it for the five years it took to get a deed free and clear. Besides, rich deposits of coal had been discovered all across North Dakota, solving the problem of how to keep warm on the treeless, windswept veldt, where winter temperatures often dropped lower than thermometers could register. True, the coal was only soft lignite, but it burned nearly as hot as the hard bituminous coal once you got it going.

The event that began moving would-be farmers into the northwestern part of the state, however, was the coming of the Minneapolis, Saint Paul, and Sault Ste. Marie Railroad, nicknamed the Soo Line. In 1893 the Soo Line had extended its reach into the western edge of North Dakota, laying 182 miles of new track. Now immigrants could flow into the area more easily and coal, grain, and cattle could be shipped to Eastern markets.

Land developer Eli C. Tolley lost no time in claiming large tracts of land around Middle Des Lacs Lake, then printing flyers and placing newspaper ads that extolled the virtues of the surrounding counties. *Free Lands! Farming Lands! Dairy Lands! Grazing Lands! Hay Lands! Coal!* the advertisements boasted

UNCLE JOHN'S STORY

in German, Swedish, Norwegian, and English. What the ads didn't mention was that Tolley had also shot and killed the first postmaster and sole resident of Lignite. The postmaster, a dugout-living squatter named Augustine Rouse, didn't care for Tolley's encroachment on his town of one. As a respected representative of the Minnesota Loan and Trust Company of Minneapolis, however, Tolley had been able to bull his way out of jail after the murder and continue his town-building.

That was three years ago, Uncle John said, and the growing community of Lignite had been renamed Kenmare. Some folks said that Tolley had created the name from the Gaelic words *ken mair:* meaning *to know more.* Others claimed that when Tolley's wife first glimpsed the town along the lakeshore, she exclaimed that it reminded her of Kenmare, Ireland. However the town's name had come about, groups of Danes, Swedes, Dunkards, and Amish–Mennonites soon arrived by rail and covered wagon, broke the heavy sod, and planted crops.

Unfortunately, last year's crops had been destroyed by a July hailstorm, which battered much of the standing grain into the ground. Then, in fall, an enormous prairie fire raged for three days and ravaged twenty square miles.

Uncle John described how thick smoke obscured the sun day after day as farmers frantically plowed fire breaks, set backfires, and sloshed well water onto their wooden shanties and outbuildings. Luckily, many homes were "soddies," built from thick bricks of prairie sod, and those did not burn. But the winter's supply of hay for the stock and the cash crop of grain were gone. After the fire snuffed itself out the naked, blackened prairie resembled a newly plowed field as far in every direction as one could see.

Edd listened breathlessly as Uncle John told how huge buffalo wolves roamed the deep coulees and howled through the prairie nights, chasing the ghosts of the nearly extinct bison, whose majestic bones now littered the ground. Springtime and autumn shrilled with the clamor of geese, ducks, brants, and other migrating waterfowl, as millions of wings darkened the seemingly endless reach of sapphire sky. And winter brought bone-numbing cold and deep snowdrifts; sometimes hard-driving winds would scour the prairie clean, then the next blizzard would howl out of the northwest and dump several more feet of the dry, icy crystals.

"There's nothing easy about life in that country," Uncle John said, "but the prairie is wide open and free, and somehow it gets a grip on you. And it seems like there's a fine bunch of folks settling around Kenmare. So we'll try for a crop of wheat this year and see how it goes," he finished, smiling at Mattie.

That night in bed Edd was wakeful, as visions of wind-blown grasslands, sod homes, wolves, buffalo bones, and lush fields of oats and wheat tumbled through his mind. Newly settled places offered opportunities for men who weren't afraid to work, and he was no stranger to hard labor. But he was more than three years away from twenty-one and by rights he owed those years to his Pa, even if Pa did let him work for the neighbors when opportunity arose. Gradually, however, Edd's mind formed a plan to gain his freedom. He resolved to consider all the details carefully and then talk with his father when the time seemed right.

UNCLE JOHN'S STORY

Edd and his older sister, Lyddy, who helped raise him.

CHAPTER 4: Freedom Bound

As the steam locomotive chuffed slowly out of the station at Bellefontaine, Ohio, Edd shoved the window open and waved goodbye to Pa, who had driven him to the depot, and to sister Ola Mae, who'd come along to see him off. As the train picked up speed, Ola Mae's waving white handkerchief faded into his last glimpse of the town.

Edd settled his well-built, five-foot-eleven-inch frame onto the red plush seat and breathed deeply to calm himself. At last he was bound for North Dakota! The Ohio countryside flew by the windows at forty miles per hour as Edd recalled the conversation that had gained him his freedom.

On the Monday after Uncle John regaled the family with stories of Dakota, John's daughter, Fannie, married Lewis Morningstar, and the couple planned to travel to Kenmare with John and Mattie to begin their married life on a new homestead claim. John's son Levi and Levi's wife, Rebecca, were going, too. Everyone was headed West, it seemed, and Edd lost no time in enlisting Uncle John's help to convince Pa that Edd should go, too.

"If I get Pa to agree to let me set out on my own before I'm twenty-one, can you use some help on your farm?" Edd asked Uncle John.

John stroked his beard while he thought about it. "Well," he considered, "now that my sons Levi and Daniel are married, and Joseph and Willie are still too young to work in the fields, you'd be right welcome. I could put in a bigger crop of grain this year and maybe build a sod barn, and you could help with the harvesting, too. If you can convince your Pa that he doesn't need you on the farm this year, I'll tell him you can stay with us in return for work," he said.

The next evening, after the chores were done, Edd found Pa in the barn settling the horses for the night.

"Pa, I've been thinking," Edd eased into his topic. "I work more for the neighbors than here at home now that Frank and Dan are old enough to help out. I know I'm beholden to give you my time until I'm twenty-one, but Uncle John says he could use my help this year to get his farm going, and I wondered whether you might let me strike out on my own and work for him." Edd paused to let the idea sink in a little and then he offered the kicker: "If you were to favor the idea, I'd turn my inheritance over to you."

Big, strapping Ezra set the horses' feed bucket down and turned his full-bearded face to meet Edd's clear, blue-eyed gaze. He considered the proposal for what seemed like a long time before he spoke.

"Your mother wanted you and Lyddy to have five-hundred dollars each to start out with when you were twenty-one," he reminded Edd. "She knew she was dying, so giving you that chance was the best she could do for you. She set real store by the idea." He paused. "I admit, I could make good use of the money in these depressed times, but if you give up your inheritance now you might find hard going later on and regret it."

Ezra saw the set of Edd's jaw and noted the determination in the young man's face.

"I see that your mind's made up, son, but I'll have to pray about it and talk with John and with Mother Lydia."

Edd knew better than to push the idea further, so he thanked Pa and left the barn.

It was hard to wait out the few days it took Pa to consider Edd's plan, but by the end of the week, it was settled: Edd would help Pa with the early spring work and then leave for Dakota, where the spring thaw came later than in Ohio. He would board with Uncle John and Aunt Mattie, and when John didn't need his help, Edd could hire out to other homesteaders.

Before he left West Liberty, Edd signed a paper releasing his five-hundred-dollar inheritance to Pa. Now he was his own man, free to make his life what he would.

Edward's mother, Nancy A. (Zook) Yoder

CHAPTER 5: In the Hollow of God's Hand

Before he left Ohio, Edd paid a visit to his paternal grandparents. One afternoon he found himself alone with his father's unmarried sister, Fannie, who still lived at home. They sat in the parlor talking about family and looking at a few photographs Fannie had tucked into an album.

"I have something for you, Edd, and this seems like a good time to give it to you," Fannie remarked. She carefully extracted a small photograph from the album and handed it to him. "This is a picture of your real mother and, as far as I know, it's the only one that exists," she said.

Stunned, Edd looked down at the sweet likeness he held in his hand as his Aunt Fannie continued.

"You know, while your mother was alive she took to heart the church's teachings against photographs — the making of a 'graven image.' She asked that all images of her be destroyed and your father did as she asked. But I loved Nancy dearly and I kept this one picture of her, thinking that someday her children would want to see what their mother looked like when she was young."

A flood of feelings rushed through Edd and the one that surfaced first was anger.

"Now that I am on my own, I will never be a member of the

Mennonite church," he cried. "It has too many hypocrites who say one thing and do another, and I will never forget how poorly I've been treated by some in the community. As long as I live a moral life, I don't need or want *any* church telling me what to do." He paused and took a deep breath, but failed to keep his voice from trembling as he went on. "I'm glad, *glad* you kept this picture; I thank you for it, and I will treasure it. I have wondered so many times what my mother was like and what she thought of me."

Aunt Fannie was taken aback by Edd's outburst, but her heart went out to this young man, still so much a child in some ways, a determined adult in others, ready to set out into a world he knew little about. She looked at him searchingly and then she said quietly,

"Your mother loved you very much, and she was so terribly sad at leaving you. She would be sorry to hear that you feel so about the church. Her constant concern was that you would be well cared for and that you would grow up to love God and be a worthy member of the Mennonite community."

Edd's eyes dropped to the photograph again as Fannie continued speaking.

"Every day, every single day in the weeks before she died, your mother would ask that you be brought to her bedside, and she held you in her arms and prayed for you. She prayed that God would keep you always in the hollow of His hand."

The room was silent for a time, and when Edd finally raised his eyes to meet Aunt Fannie's, tears streaked his face.

"I miss her so much," he said, "even though I never knew her.

IN THE HOLLOW OF GOD'S HAND

I will miss her all my life. Your telling me how she felt about me does me so much good, I can't begin to thank you enough."

"Wherever you go, whatever life brings you, always remember that those who have loved you are with you in some way," Aunt Fannie said, "and that God is watching over you."

The Soo railroad line opened up the Dakota prairies to homesteaders. Eli C. Tolley's Land Office can be seen in the background, and Soo Line immigrant cars line up along Kenmare's railroad tracks.

The town square, Kenmare, North Dakota.

CHAPTER 6: Immigrant Train

A BURGEONING SPRING LANDSCAPE unfolded outside the train windows as the Chicago, Milwaukee & St. Paul Railroad cars steamed northwestward, from Chicago's bustling streets through the dense forests of Wisconsin and Minnesota. When Edd changed to the Soo Line in Minneapolis, he saw that the engine pulled many immigrant cars: boxcars rented by westbound families to transport livestock, household goods, and farming implements. A father or sometimes an older son rode for free in the immigrant car with the livestock, but the rest of the family must pay for seats in a passenger car. It wasn't unusual to see women with seven, eight, or more children camped out in a third-class compartment, sleeping stretched out on seats or even on the floor if the train was crowded.

Edd eagerly absorbed each new sight and sound, striking up conversations with other westbound travelers and lending a willing ear to tall pioneering tales. People gravitated to the good-looking, mannerly fellow's honest expression, piercing blue eyes, and ready smile.

Near Minnesota's western border the forest gave way to open grasslands: flat terrain that increasingly curved into rounded landforms as the long train stretched its way into North Dakota. Edd stared out the window at a bleak, yet somehow haunting landscape shimmering with indigo pools of snowmelt surrounded by tall, golden stalks of dried grasses. Scores of birds flew up from the pools as the train rumbled past: ducks, geese, grebes, trumpeter swans, and many others Edd could not identify.

Northwest of Lakota, deep fissures cracked the earth, revealing only the tops of a few stunted trees. Those fissures were called coulees, Edd's seatmate explained, and they drained water off the grasslands and sheltered a wealth of plant and animal life. Above the coulees' mysterious mouths the land rose and bent and curved in seemingly never-ending flow beneath a shockingly wide vault of sky. Although the sun streamed through puffy clouds directly above the train, Edd watched a spring thunderstorm blacken the sky miles to the southwest. Lightening forked out of that blackness again and again as cloud shadows ate up the prairie. A deep blue rain curtain billowed across the land, caught the train in its folds, and rushed away to the northeast as the storm's

IMMIGRANT TRAIN

main thrust passed south of them.

North of Minot the terrain grew increasingly hilly, its folds draining into marshland that ultimately became the Des Lacs Lakes. At last, late in the afternoon, the Soo Line's railcars ground into Kenmare and disgorged their exhausted cargo. Edd helped some of the woman and children climb down the train's steep steps, and families huddled near the tracks waiting for fathers and older brothers to join them from their billets in the freight cars.

Newly built wooden immigrant sheds loomed rawly behind the depot: the Soo Line had erected two, three-hundred-foot-long buildings for families to camp in for a few days while their menfolk claimed land and threw up wood-and-tar-paper shanties or muscled up a soddie. To save time, shanties often were built on skids, in town, and sledded to the claims.

The Kenmare immigrant sheds were partitioned into rooms and entire families squeezed into a ten- by twenty-foot space. Still, those folks were better off than the pioneers who'd arrived two years earlier, when twelve-hundred immigrant cars unloaded at Kenmare and many families were forced to live in their rented boxcars until they could move to a homestead.

Behind the sheds, the steel-gray sweep of Middle Des Lacs Lake spread shallowly for several square miles. A normally sluggish river, now swollen with melted snow, linked the lake to Upper Des Lacs Lake to the north and Lower Des Lacs Lake to the south. The immigrants hauled lake water for drinking, cooking, and washing clothes and bodies, and they shot waterfowl to supplement the food staples they'd brought with them on the train. But the primitive living conditions they found on arrival were only a prelude to the hardships of establishing a home in this treeless land and harsh climate.

Uncle John met Edd at the depot and the two men climbed into John's wagon for a quick tour of the town. Kenmare was laid out around a central square, which the city planners intended would become a park. Twelve businesses, including dry goods, furniture, and hardware stores, plus a bank, newspaper office, livery barn, lumber yard, and machine shed lined one side of the wide main street on the lake side of the square. A long hitching rail ran down the other side of the street; beyond that, a few houses scattered across the prairie like a handful of children's blocks, carelessly tossed. Along other sides of the square a new hotel was going up and several other buildings were under construction. Although Edd did not know it, he was viewing a one-time snapshot of the town: within weeks, half of the businesses would be destroyed by fire, including the town's first newspaper, the two-month-old *Kenmare Journal*.

As Uncle John drove the horses south from Kenmare toward his claim, Edd marveled at the thousands of spring flowers carpeting the ground: long-stemmed violets, pasque flowers, buttercups, and crocus nodded among the grasses. John told him that wild strawberries and prairie roses would soon follow. Along the railroad tracks, which paralleled the river, the air was thick with waterfowl on spring migration to their Canada breeding grounds. Occasionally the men spied sharptail grouse and prairie chickens in the vegetation along the river. A few more miles south, a large herd of longhorn cattle grazed on the McBride

IMMIGRANT TRAIN

ranch, and further along lay Lower Des Lacs Lake, where Uncle John stopped to rest the horses and shoot a brace of ducks.

The sun had long since set by the time the men reached the Kauffmans' soddie, a huddled black shape in the starlight. Although the low-ceilinged prairie home was cramped inside, Aunt Mattie had scattered colorful rag rugs on its floor, the beds boasted bright quilts, and red-checked oilcloth covered the roughhewn table. A fire in the cast-iron cook stove kept the thick-walled house almost too warm, but spring nights in Dakota could be bitterly cold, and Edd was thankful to be inside the cozy, lighted building. Almost too tired to speak, he ate the supper Mattie had kept hot for him and gratefully tumbled into bed.

Early pioneers often built prairie homes and stables of sod bricks. Tough grass roots held the sod together, and the thick walls blocked the ever-present prairie winds, keeping the building's interior cool in summer and warm in winter.

CHAPTER 7: Dakota Days

COOL SPRING DAYS YIELDED TO SUMMER'S HEAT as Edd helped Uncle John plow one hundred and sixty acres of fire-blackened sod and seed it with oats, wheat, and alfalfa. The men wrestled the unbroken ground using walking plows fitted with razor-sharp prairie-breaker blades and pulled by burly, slow-moving oxen. As the plow blades sliced through densely rooted grasses, turning over long strips of sod, the men "harvested" some of those strips and stacked them to make a low-roofed shelter for the stock. Ground that had been broken in earlier years was turned over using either horses or oxen hitched to a walking plow carrying a general-purpose blade. Few settlers owned riding plows, and at day's end the men staggered exhaustedly to their sod homes and shanties, ravenously hungry, yet almost too tired to eat.

Compared with the mellow, well-tilled soil of his Ohio home, Edd found the cantankerous prairie sod almost impossibly unyielding, but his strong young body bent to the task willfully and with an increasing sense of accomplishment. When spring planting was finished at Kauffmans', Edd worked on a nearby farm for five dollars a month and board, breaking ground for next year's planting, scything and stacking the tall prairie grasses for cattle fodder, and doing general farm labor.

The Dakota country was everything Edd had imagined it would be and more, but that didn't change the fact that wrestling a living from it was going to take time, determination, and ingenuity. Until farmers could make their first good crop, cash money was in short supply. Ironically, it was the buffalo — a primary source of food, shelter, and clothing for the Plains Indians, but long since wantonly destroyed by the white man — that now came to the rescue. While their menfolk plowed and planted, women and children collected gunnysacks full of buffalo bones, which were shipped back East by the freight-car load to be carved into knife handles and ground into fertilizer.

The buffalo had left another, more frightening legacy. Deprived of their traditional prey, one-hundred-fifty-pound buffalo wolves stalked the longhorn cattle that some immigrants — trying to make a go of ranching rather than farming — pastured on their homesteads. Wolves killed a dozen out of every hundred cattle and dug through the roofs of sod barns to attack other livestock as well, causing the desperate settlers to join forces and offer a dollar-per-head wolf bounty.

Keeping warm could be a trial, too. Although deposits of the soft lignite coal were plentiful, the coal required wood chips to start it burning, and wood was an almost nonexistent commodity. Homesteaders scoured the coulees, gleaning even the tiniest sticks and bits of brushwood. When that kindling source was exhausted, they gathered dried cow dung, which burned readily, or twisted dried grass into hay sticks to make a quick, hot fire.

Those challenges, added to grass fires and crop-destroying

DAKOTA DAYS

Construction of the railroads across the Great Plains was the beginning of the willful extermination of the buffalo. Thirty-one million animals were wantonly killed and left to rot in Kansas alone. Later, settlers collected buffalo bones and shipped train-car loads east to be made into fertilizer, knife handles, and various trinkets.

storms, drained the emotional and monetary resources of many settlers long before they could begin to make a living from the defiant land. But Edd quickly grew to love the prairie's wide vistas, its dramatic storms, and the rich black soil hidden beneath its fibrous grass cover. He began to believe that he could make a life in this place.

Edd turned eighteen that summer and the hard toil and rough living conditions toughened his body and matured his mind even as they freed his spirit from the constraints of his Ohio childhood. Although he had attended school only through eighth grade, Edd continued to educate himself and keep abreast of current events. After the May 1899 fire destroyed its two-month-old building and equally new printing press, the proprietors of the *Kenmare Journal* rented a building, purchased a used press, and continued churning out a weekly paper. Edd bought or borrowed a copy of the *Journal* whenever he could. Despite his meager wages, he never begrudged the cost.

Fall brought a poor harvest, but the settlers gathered what grain they could and hunkered down for the harsh winter. Because the cold months offered little work and he would be another mouth for Uncle John to feed, Edd traveled back to Ohio to spend the winter with his family. But the prairie had fired his blood, and all winter the land called for his return. Disappointingly, Uncle John wrote in June to say that severe drought through the winter and spring made good crops unlikely that year, so Edd stayed in Ohio. But the following year he again journeyed to North Dakota and hired out as a day laborer to the Sharp, Hostetler, Kauffman, and Morningstar families, quickly gaining a reputation as a good-humored, willing worker.

When Edd returned to North Dakota in the spring of 1901, he found that a Mennonite community had formed near a new railroad spur in the hills south of Kenmare. The homesteaders had named the little settlement Baden, after a town in Germany. A young couple named Lundt opened a combination grocery store, butcher shop, and post office near the tracks; a one-room schoolhouse and a grain elevator were soon built; and coal could be obtained from a coulee fifteen miles to the east. Pioneer life began to stabilize, allowing time and opportunity for socializing, and Edd quickly became a welcome addition to jolly Sunday gatherings of young people and occasional weekday evenings at the store spinning yarns or playing checkers.

The first bumper crop of wheat and oats matured on the farms around Kenmare and Baden in 1901: a breathtaking, golden wealth of grain that demanded machine harvesting. Locally, a few young men formed a threshing crew and acquired a steam-powered harvester, hauling it from farm to farm to separate grain from straw in return for a percentage of the crop. The threshers recruited Edd, making this the first of seven years that he would join the hardy gangs who worked from before dawn until moonrise, seven days a week, for more than a month, racing to get the settlers' grain harvested and under cover before the first snowfall.

Threshing paid well — so well that it attracted men from across the United States and Canada, many of whom bummed rides on freight cars to get to the grain belt of the Dakotas, Iowa, Kansas, and Nebraska. When the year's work came to an end, Edd had a pocketful of money and a body leaned down to pure muscle. He wintered in Ohio once more, but when he headed west again the following spring he was not to see his home state or family again for five years. Several times he would come within a single breath of never seeing them again.

Edd's reputation as an honest, upright young man and a hardy laborer assured him a job in North Dakota in the spring of 1902. From April through October he earned twenty-four dollars plus his room, board, and washing working on the farm of a Scottish family: the Norman Hickaleers. The family treated Edd like one of their own, the four children adopting him as an older brother, and for the rest of his life Edd tempered his experiences with the old Scotsman's favorite saying in any crisis, large or small: "Take it aisy, son, just take it aisy."

But after years of toiling for others, the most important event of his adult life thus far was about to occur. In July, Edd turned twenty-one, making him eligible to file a homestead claim of his own.

CHAPTER 8: Free Land

FREE LAND WAS BECOMING SCARCE near the town of Kenmare. The town had incorporated in 1901, new businesses multiplied and flourished, and each year the population doubled. Edd watched anxiously as section after section sprouted a claim shanty and the grassland was plowed into cropland.

One October day, Cousin Lee Kauffman rode his horse into the Hickaleers' farmyard bringing exciting news. A neighbor had pulled up stakes and gone back East, and his unimproved forty acres had reverted to the government. Lee had heard the news before it was posted in the *Journal* because the property adjoined his claim.

Knowing he must act quickly, Edd took the next day off and borrowed a horse to ride out and look the acreage over. The claim was well positioned: four miles south of Kenmare and a mile west of Lower Des Lacs Lake. It also was close to six hundred and forty acres of designated school land, where short-grass hay could be harvested by anyone with the initiative to do so. And it was near Uncle John's farm, the Lundt's store at Baden, and the railway line.

Claims must be filed at the land office in Minot, so Edd walked to Kenmare and took the train south to the bustling capitol city.

On Wednesday, October 22, he paid the required six-dollar filing fee and agreed to establish residence on the homestead and improve the land for five years. If he kept his part of the bargain, the forty acres would then be his.

Jubilant, Edd boarded the train to return to Kenmare, scarcely believing that at last he would have a farm of his own. As the train steamed north, however, his excitement waned as he soberly considered how much money he would need to build a shanty and outbuildings, as well as to buy tools and seed for spring planting. To raise his spirits, Edd struck up a conversation with a robust Scandinavian in the seat across from him. The strapping Swede was headed for the pinewoods of Minnesota to spend the winter lumbering, and for the next two hours he regaled Edd with his exploits as a lumberjack.

"A man can make good money in the woods," the Swede bragged. "The lumber companies are paying thirty to thirty-five dollars a month for unskilled labor, plus room and board and a round-trip train ticket." That was all-time-record pay, he said, but the timber magnates had big lumber orders to fill and the mills were running twenty-four hours a day, seven days a week.

Edd questioned the burly Scandinavian thoroughly and learned which companies might be hiring that winter and how long the jobs were likely to last.

"Freeze-up usually comes in November and lasts through March or April," the Swede related. "That's when it's easiest to haul logs out o' the woods. But a few 'jacks are kept on into summer to drive the logs down the rivers. Some fellows work on farms during the summer and fall and go to the woods for the winter and spring," he said.

As the train chugged into the station at Kenmare the Swede offered some parting advice. "If you're ever on the bum looking for work and you need to know anything at all about a place, ask a saloon keeper," he said. "They know who's hiring, and they can give you directions or tell you where to find a bed for the night." Edd thanked the lumberjack for his counsel and the men parted, the Swede to continue north to the pineries and Edd to return to his final week of working for the Hickaleers.

As October drew to a close, Edd thought hard about his options. He had promised the government that he'd live on his homestead claim at least six months of each year, but he hadn't yet established residency and he needed money to do so. If he went to the woods, he could earn enough to build a claim shanty and buy seed and tools plus food and other necessities to make it through spring planting. He decided it was worth a try. When he left the Hickaleer farm, he would travel to the lumber camps the Swede had told him about near Bemidji, Minnesota, and see whether he could get a winter job. It was a decision that would nearly cost him his life.

Third Street in Bemidji, Minnesota, shortly before the town's incorporation as the Beltrami County Seat. The lake shore can be seen at the far end of the street. Bemidji soon became the roughest lumber town in the state, boasting sixty-two saloons and seven houses of ill-repute.

CHAPTER 9: Bemidji-gu-mog

MINNESOTA'S TIMBER WAS RAPIDLY DISAPPEARING beneath the combined onslaught of farmers and lumbermen. In the southwestern part of the state, would-be farmers felled the Big Woods: five thousand square miles of oak, maple, hickory, black walnut, and butternut. They piled the logs high and doused the pyres with kerosene. Determined to plant wheat, the immigrants burned and grubbed the forest out by the roots, forever altering a landscape rich in natural resources.

East of the Mississippi, the North Woods — or pineries — marched all the way to the Canadian border. In a region larger than the state of Maine a coniferous forest of white pine, Norway pine, jack pine, spruce, cedar, tamarack, and balsam laid its fragrant shadow across the land. The region's acidic soil held little appeal for farmers, but the kingly white pine drew lumbermen like a magnet. Minnesota's magnificent system of rivers and lakes became the first lumber highways, but iron rails followed hot on the timber barons' heels. Soon a network of railroads sent the state's wealth of pine everywhere that nation-building demanded it. Within fifty years, Minnesota's thirty-eight million acres of hardwoods and pinewoods would be gone.

Much of the desirable white pine stood on the Red Lake and

White Earth reservations — land that had been promised to the Ojibwa/Chippewa Indians. As the forests surrounding those reserves were cut, the nation cast a greedy eye on the Indians' timber. Interested parties crafted a plan to herd all nonreservation Chippewa onto the White Earth Reservation, deed each adult a certain number of acres, and open the rest to lumbering. The Red Lake Reservation also was to be logged.

In 1888 the Carson brothers established a trading post on the south shore of Lake Bemidji-gu-mog: an Indian moniker that described the lake's oblique shape. The Carsons aimed to establish commerce with nearby Native American settlements: Leech Lake Reservation to the west, White Earth to the east, and Red Lake to the north. A decade later the Great Northern Railroad laid tracks along the shore and built a depot, the trading post grew into a settlement and, seemingly overnight, the settlement became a town.

By 1897 Bemidji was incorporated and established as the county seat. Boasting sixty-two saloons and seven houses of ill repute, it soon became the roughest lumber town in the state and the second roughest in the nation (Butte, Montana, held dubious first place). Lumberjacks could easily lose a month's pay in one evening: if the taverns and prostitutes — known as LumberJills — didn't take their money, roving gangs of thieves would. And lives were lost as easily as money. Dead bodies, stripped of valuables and even clothing, frequently turned up in the brush along the lakeshore.

When Edd stepped off the train at Bemidji in the winter of 1902, the frigid dusk closed in around him. Several feet of new snow

BEMIDJI-GU-MOG

Passengers disembark at the train depot in Bemidji, Minnesota. A coal car rests on a siding at left.

blanketed the ground on either side of the tracks and cast an eerie glow on the unpainted warehouses that loomed around the wood-frame depot, which anchored the south end of town. A block to the east, a ghostly fog rose from Lake Bemidji's still-unfrozen waters. Edd turned up his coat collar, picked up his battered suitcase, and began walking along the lakeshore toward the town's center. His heavy boots crunched through a hard crust of snow to the fluffy layer beneath and his breath clouded before his face.

Edd had taken only a few steps when he happened to glance behind him. Three rough-looking men, last seen leaning against the station wall, were shoving their way through the small crowd on the platform. As Edd kept walking, he heard the slow crunch of their footsteps coming along behind him. He walked a little faster and the footsteps kept pace. Edd began to feel afraid, for three against one were poor odds.

I'll bet they're going to try to rob me, he thought.

Quickly he turned away from the lake and headed down Third Street, where several lighted buildings beckoned. One unpainted building bore the sign Bank Saloon, and remembering the burly Swede's advice on the train from Minot, Edd gratefully ducked through the saloon's door.

The noisy, smoke-filled room reeked of stale beer and sweaty bodies, but Edd walked up to the bar and set his suitcase down on the splintery wooden floor. He took a deep breath and waited patiently until the grizzled bartender stopped in front of him and swiped at the bar with a none-too-clean rag. Edd returned the bartender's friendly nod, then asked,

"Can you tell me if any of the lumber camps are hiring?"

"Sure, sure," the bartender spoke rapidly, out of habit. "I've heard Crookston's is taking on 'jacks, mebbe the Brainerd Lumber Company, too. And you might ask for work at Steidl's sawmill."

The bartender told Edd where the mill was located and how to contact the local employment agents, who charged men one dollar to place them in the camps. Then he advised:

"If I was you, son, I'd get a room for the night at the Merchant's Hotel, a block over on Second Street, and stay put 'till morning. Now what'll you have to drink?"

Still somewhat shaken, Edd thanked the man for his help and ordered a whiskey. He'd never tasted alcohol before but it seemed like a good time to try it. Surely a drink would settle his nerves. The bartender placed a shot glass on the bar and filled it three-quarters full, then moved away to help another customer.

Edd raised the glass to his lips, but before he could sip the clear liquid he felt the firm yet soft pressure of a hand on his right shoulder. Surprised, he turned his head, only to find that no one stood near enough to touch him. Suddenly, from head to foot, his body was swept with the absolute conviction that the hand that had rested so softly on his shoulder was his mother's — a hand whose touch he had not felt since he was five months old. Unbidden, he remembered his Aunt Fannie's words: "Your mother prayed that you would grow up to be a worthy member of the Mennonite community. She prayed that God would keep you always in the hollow of His hand."

Slowly, Edd set the untouched glass of whisky on the bar, picked up his suitcase, and left the saloon.

Lumberjacks haul white pine over ice roads in the Minnesota woods.

CHAPTER 10: The North Woods

AFTER A RESTLESS NIGHT, Edd ate a hearty breakfast served family-style in the hotel dining room, then strode determinedly through the lobby doors to meet the day head-on. Daylight showed Bemidji's mean streets at a disadvantage; the shabby, unpainted wooden buildings surrounded by dirty snow banks exuded neither civic pride nor permanence. Undaunted by his crude surroundings, Edd canvassed the employment agents and soon landed a job as a lumberjack. The agent who hired him planned to take newly hired 'jacks out to the camp later that day and told Edd to come back to the office after lunch.

Having a few hours to wait, Edd tramped the snow-packed dirt streets until he came to E. H. Winter's dry goods store. Inside the store he questioned the clerk closely about the type of gear he would need for working in the woods.

"You can buy your supplies at the camp store — the 'wanigan'," salesman Henry Miller told him, "but they'll cost you the earth."

Congratulating himself on his foresight, at Miller's recommendation Edd bought extra wool socks and mittens, high-topped woodsman's moccasins or "larrigans," extra-large overalls, a thick plaid mackinaw, a warm cap with earflaps, and several heavy woolen blankets. He rolled his new clothing up in the blankets and left the roll and his suitcase with the desk clerk at the hotel, then continued his walk through town.

A long dock, consisting of wide planks laid three abreast and resting on log pilings, extended from the end of Third Street far out into the lake. To the left of the dock the warehouses of the Viking Boat Works squatted on the shore. Edd walked gingerly onto the planks, which were coated with icy vapor from the rapidly freezing lake, and looked out across a broad expanse of water, gray beneath a lowering gray sky. It was a sight to make a man feel lonely and insignificant. Remembering his experiences of the previous evening, Edd shivered with something more than cold as he turned and made his way back into town.

Later that day, the lumber company's wagon slipped and slid for hours over the frozen ruts of the woods road, often nearly unseating the men with its gyrations. Edd lost track of time as the wagon rolled deeper and deeper into the forest, and dusk had cloaked the landscape when at last the men saw lights glimmering through the trees. The agent pointed out landmarks as they drove through the camp. A long, squat log building roofed with tarpaper and lath proved to be the bunkhouse. Another log structure standing at right angles to the first was the kitchen, dining hall, and storeroom or "dingle." Across the road, several smaller buildings housed the blacksmith shop, combination office–wanigan, saw filer's shop, granary, and hay shed. Behind those, a row of barns sheltered the camp's horses and equipment.

As the men piled out of the wagon, Foreman "Windy" Carver — so named because he talked fast and long — introduced himself, then turned the would-be 'jacks over to the head cook, known as the "bull-cook," who would assign each man his bunk. The bull-cook led them into a building designed to accommodate forty men. Stark and functional, the bunkhouse walls were smoke-darkened peeled logs; unvarnished wooden planks formed the floor. Two tiers of side-loader bunks, which resembled continuous shelves with sides, ran around three walls of the big room. A tiny window at each gable end and a skylight near the middle of the roof furnished ventilation. Edd noticed that the cavernous space was lit by a single kerosene lantern, but two cast-iron box stoves held court in the center of the floor, and a long table stood between them.

In between the stoves and the bunks, rough-hewn wooden slabs on short legs formed a long "deacon seat" where the men sat to pull on socks and boots in the morning or tell stories after the evening meal. On the front wall, roller towels flanked a water barrel and several large wash sinks. Wires for hanging up wet socks, mittens, and other clothing were strung a few feet below the roof. Finally, a door in the back wall opened onto a path that led to the outhouses.

Edd was assigned an upper bunk — less desirable because clothing and other possessions must be stored in the bunk itself rather than beneath it — then the bull-cook told them, "Each man gets a fresh half-bale of straw from the hay shed to spread in his bunk. Supper's in one hour when the cookee blows the horn. Lights out at nine o'clock. Teamsters rise at four o'clock, 'jacks rise at four-thirty, and breakfast is at five. Go to it."

The men trouped across the road to the hay shed and carefully

IN THE HOLLOW OF GOD'S HAND

A cookee blows his six-foot-long horn to signal Sunday dinner time, as lumberjacks file into the dining hall. The sound of the horn carried for miles through the woods.

chose the cleanest looking straw bales. Back in the bunkhouse, Edd mounded the sweet-smelling straw into the box-sided pine bunk and tucked a wool blanket over it. He placed his remaining two blankets on top for covers. If a man wanted a pillow, he folded a shirt or a pair of overalls beneath his head. Each man placed his baggage in the bunk at his head and his neighbor's baggage sat at his feet, forming divisions between sleepers. No man was allowed to sit or lounge in another's bunk, which would be "home" for the six-month winter logging season.

No sooner had Edd settled his belongings than a sonorous horn

THE NORTH WOODS

blast announced the evening meal. As he filed into the dining hall with the others, Edd noted with surprise that the men fell silent and each seemed to have his particular place at the long, trestle tables. The new men waited until the bull-cook assigned them places, then seated themselves on backless pine benches. Kerosene lanterns hanging from the rafters threw a fitful light over the plain furnishings and reflected off the tin dishes. At each place, a large metal bowl rested upside down on a turned-over pie plate, which in turn covered a set of eating utensils.

The cooks set large bowls of fried salt pork, boiled beef, beans, potatoes, and plates of homemade bread on the table, followed by dried applesauce or stewed prunes, rice pudding, cookies, and doughnuts. They filled the men's cups again and again with strong tea. Edd noticed that silence was the rule at the table and the men ate heartily but quickly, consuming the entire meal in about twenty minutes. When finished, they did not linger, but quietly rose and walked back to the bunkhouse.

Edd listened more than he talked that evening, for he had much to learn about lumbering. Tired after his restless night at the hotel, he was glad when lights-out came at nine o'clock. All too soon he heard the stove doors clatter as the bull-cook built up the fire, then the first wake-up call roused the teamsters: "Roooooll out!" He burrowed deeper into his warm blankets and dozed until the cookee blew a shrill blast on his six-foot-long horn. In the clear, cold morning, the sound rang through the woods for miles.

Edd watched how the other men dressed and followed their lead, pulling on heavy long underwear, a thick shirt and woolen pants, three or four pairs of socks stretched up over the bottom of his pants, the extra-large overalls on top of everything, then the high-topped larrigans, plaid mackinaw, mittens, and cap. The 'jacks could only guess at how cold it was outdoors. The camp owners would not allow thermometers on the premises, believing that the truth would discourage the men from working. But however cold it was, every man peeled off his mackinaw once the heavy work got underway. Only slackers, who failed to work up a sweat, wore jackets during the workday.

Breakfast was another huge meal. The men tackled mountains of buckwheat pancakes, piles of pork hash, and hefty bowls of molasses-laced beans, washed down with cups of strong coffee, followed by platters of doughnuts, then more coffee sweetened with brown sugar. After breakfast a few of the men smoked pipes or chewed "baccy" as they readied their equipment and waited for sunrise.

Timber was cut and sleigh-hauled in winter when much of the forest undergrowth had died back; the vicious blackflies, mosquitoes, and ticks were gone; and the huge logs could be easily sledded to the lakeshore or railroad siding on ice roads.

First the foreman and timber cruiser mapped out a tote road that ran from the stand to be cut to the shipping area. Roads were laid out along creek bottoms or swamps whenever possible to avoid hills, then leveled and graded in September or October while the ground was dry. As soon as freezing weather came to stay, horses pulled water tanks — large wooden boxes on sled runners — to the road, and the men began building up layer after layer of ice.

THE NORTH WOODS

By December, when log hauling began, a foot of ice coated the grade and the foreman sent a "rut cutter" out to score parallel ruts four inches deep and seven and a half feet apart to keep the sled runners on the track. Lumberjacks designated as "road monkeys" repaired the ruts when necessary and kept the road free of horse dung. After a snowstorm, the men plowed and tramped the road solid, then the icing and rut cutting were repeated. Meanwhile, brush cutters, sawyers, and choppers cleared the undergrowth and felled and limbed the tall pines. Lumberjacks known as "skidders" hitched oxen to each log and towed it to the road while "swampers" bushwacked a trail ahead of them, then they loaded the logs onto sleds. Teamsters hitched four or more horses to a sled and pulled as many as fifty logs at a time over the slick roadbeds to a railway or water landing.

Edd worked six days a week from dawn until moonrise, with a short break for dinner. The cooks hauled the noon meal of beans stewed with beef or pork to the woods in big iron kettles, and often the food froze to the tin plates before the men finished eating. The grueling labor in below-zero cold wrung every drop of energy from the men's bodies, so Edd was astonished that his comrades seemed to have an unlimited capacity for singing and storytelling around the stove in the evenings. They matched tall tales about the strongest, toughest 'jacks they had known and tried to frighten newcomers with yarns about monsters that lived in the deep woods: mythical creatures such as the tree-dwelling agropelter and the moose-headed hugag.

The agropelter was said to be a long-limbed wraith with the villainous face of an ape and arms like whiplashes that lived in trees and threw branches down on unsuspecting woodsmen, sometimes injuring them severely. The moose-headed hugag resembled a moose but had long, unjointed legs that made it impossible for the beast to lie down. As a result, it had to sleep leaning up against trees, which were sometimes pushed over by the hugag's weight.

On Sundays, the woodsmen welcomed their day in camp. After breakfast they built fires on the "boiling-up grounds" behind the bunkhouse and set iron barrels or fifty-pound lard cans full of water to heat, then took turns boiling their clothes and hanging them to freeze-dry on lines stretched between the trees. Boiling killed the ever-present lice, which Edd found to be one of the worst trials of camp life. As clean as he tried to keep himself and his clothing, the close sleeping quarters made lice impossible to avoid. Some of the men let their hair and beards grow all winter; others refused to bathe until spring. In both cases, the vermin found ample places to live and breed.

Sundays might bring a visit from one of the "sky pilots," ministers who traveled from camp to camp to wrestle the devil for the men's souls. Sky pilot Frank Higgins, a Presbyterian minister from Bemidji, was a favorite. The young, good-looking, well-spoken Higgins was a welcome sight in his heavy fur coat and woolen bill cap. He traveled the woods roads in a small box sled pulled by two enormous, shaggy dogs and the men cheered when Higgins mushed into camp, more for the news he carried from camp to camp than for any hope of salvation.

THE NORTH WOODS

Sky pilot Francis E. (Frank) Higgins was a Presbyterian minister who started a program to minister to men in the Minnesota logging camps. Higgins traveled in a box sled pulled by two enormous dogs.

Sunday also was a time for writing letters, mending clothes, reading, and catching up on sleep, but the day went by quickly and all too soon the four-thirty wake-up call came on Monday morning and another week in the woods began.

Lumberjacks pose on side-loader sleeping platforms in a Minnesota logging bunkhouse. Wet clothing was hung on lines above the bunks to dry. Edd Yoder is fifth man from lantern, top left. *The close sleeping quarters and shared roller towels in the bunkhouses fostered the spread of diseases such as smallpox.*

CHAPTER 11: Smallpox in Camp

A FEW WEEKS BEFORE CHRISTMAS, rumors of illness circulated through the lumber camp. Foreman Carver made inquiries and discovered that some of the nearby settlers had contracted the dreaded smallpox. He confined the men to camp but it was too late; one of the cookees and several of the lumberjacks were stricken. Those men were quarantined in a building known as the pest house on the outskirts of the camp and left to recover or die, as fate willed.

Edd kept working and hoped for the best, but the crowded bunkhouse with its shared roller towels and communal water dipper was a natural breeding ground for disease. One morning he awoke feeling hot and flushed, and by noon he could scarcely keep his body moving. Somehow he worked through the day, but that evening he lay in his bunk, too sick to eat dinner. The next morning, over his feeble protests, he found himself in the dreaded pest house with a score of the sick and dying. Dr. Winship, from Park Rapids, visited the camp daily to examine those who were stricken with the deadly illness, and on his next visit he examined Edd. "Open your mouth son," he commanded. And the rash on Edd's tongue confirmed the doctor's diagnosis: *smallpox*.

Within hours Edd's body was covered with the telltale red

spots and his temperature soared. For several days he feverishly tossed and turned on the hard bed, the odors of sickness, unwashed bodies, and death a miasma in the room. Each morning the bodies of those who had died were carried out and new victims took their place.

Edd's bed was by a window and on the fifth day, as he lay in a near stupor looking out at the wintry scene, he noticed a group of Indians walking up the road. One of them pulled a toboggan piled high with furs for trading at the camp store. As the Indians came abreast of the pest house the doctor, who had just arrived for his daily visit, brusquely motioned for them to move on.

"Don't you know there's sickness here?" he roared. "Half the camp is quarantined with smallpox!" One of the natives spoke to the others excitedly in their own language and they all turned and quickly headed back in the direction from which they had come.

Edd's head fell back on the pillow helplessly. He had never felt so frightened and alone. He longed for his dear sisters in Ohio and wished he could feel the softness of his mother's hand on his shoulder once again. Perhaps he would die in this awful place and no one would ever know what had become of him. But as he drifted in and out of consciousness he remembered his Aunt Fannie's sweet voice and the last words she had said to him: "Always remember that those who have loved you are with you in some way, and that God is watching over you." Then he sank into black, dreamless sleep.

How long he slept, Edd never knew, but he was awakened by

SMALLPOX IN CAMP

a cool hand on his forehead and the bustling sounds of several women moving about the room.

"Wake up, you poor dear," a woman's voice said gently, "we've brought you some Christmas dinner." He struggled to open his eyes and saw a plump, elderly woman holding a tin cup of steaming liquid.

"Here," she said, "you must be thirsty. Drink a little of this tea and then perhaps you can eat something." Throughout the room men were struggling to prop themselves up in their beds as five or six women from town handed around plates brimming with roasted turkey, potatoes and gravy, soft fresh bread, and squash pie. As sick as they were, it was hard for the men to swallow much food, but out of gratitude they made a show of eating. The hot tea tasted good and soothed Edd's sore mouth and throat. Even more comforting, however, was the knowledge that someone cared enough to risk infection just so these sick, homeless woodsmen would not feel completely abandoned on Christmas.

Although he could swallow only a few mouthfuls of the good dinner, Edd somehow knew he had turned the corner toward recovery, and that knowledge gave him the strength to endure the weeks of convalescence. His strong young body threw off the illness quickly, and by the middle of January he was able to return to work, minus an outfit of clothes, which had been burned when he was diagnosed with smallpox.

Doggedly, Edd completed the tasks the foreman assigned him, giving full value despite his weakened condition. By the end of February, however, Edd had had enough of lumbering. He was anxious to get back to his homestead claim and he had earned enough money to make the necessary improvements. He collected his pay, packed up his kit, and hitched a ride to Bemidji with a teamster.

Not wanting to spend even one more night in the squalid lumber town, Edd bought a ticket for the afternoon train and paced the depot floor as he waited for it to arrive. When the steaming engine rumbled into the station a thrilling sense of reprieve raced through his body, and he lost no time in mounting the steps of the passenger car and settling himself in a comfortable compartment. He could ride the Great Northern line all the way to Kenmare, so Edd leaned back in his seat with a sigh of relief and allowed himself to dream about spring on the prairie, the home he would one day build, and the golden fields of grain he hoped to raise.

SMALLPOX IN CAMP

During a blizzard, snow filled the railroad cutbanks, which had to be cleared by hand to allow the trains to pass.

CHAPTER 12: The Homestead

AS EDD WATCHED THROUGH THE TRAIN WINDOW, darkness settled over the frozen landscape. Suddenly the glass shuddered and turned white, obscured by the scour of wind-driven snow. Edd felt the train slow as the engineer responded to the reduced visibility. Before long the cars could do little more than creep through the whirling blizzard.

All night and all the next day the storm pummeled the train as it inched across the open prairie. A few times the engine jolted to a stop and the brakeman, tethered to a rope safety line, walked in front of it to check the rails for icing and drifts. Because the train was running against the storm, which was moving swiftly eastward, the wind had eased slightly by evening, but snow still fell thickly. In one of the cutbanks, icy crystals had drifted heavily across the tracks. Edd pulled on his heavy lumberjack clothing and helped the engineer, brakeman, and several passengers shovel the tracks clear.

Twice more before they reached Kenmare the men had to clear a cut to let the train though. When the cars finally steamed into Kenmare a day behind schedule, the eastbound trains sat, marooned on sidings, awaiting their arrival. And still the snow fell.

Edd floundered through drifts to the Arlington Hotel and

secured the last available room for the night. As he turned away from the registration desk, the front door let in a blast of cold air and his good friend, Sameuse Galyen, blew in with a swirl of snow.

"Heavens, where did you drop in from?" Sam cried, pumping Edd's hand. "We didn't expect you back until the snow melted!" Sam was shocked at Edd's gaunt appearance, but he didn't comment on it. The two friends enjoyed dinner together in the hotel dining room and Edd regaled Sam with his adventures in the North Woods.

"But, oh Sam, am I ever glad to be back," he finished. "I plan to stick around here for a good long while."

When the snow finally stopped falling, the town was buried beneath a heavy white blanket. Within days, however, a Chinook wind blew through, briefly raising the temperature to eighty degrees and melting much of the icy covering almost overnight. Edd lost no time in renting a wagon and a team of horses and hauling a load of lumber to his claim. The horses splashed through pools of snowmelt, but although flooded in places the ground was still frozen hard and the wagon rolled smoothly southward alongside the railroad tracks. Sam Galyen rode along to help unload the building materials and then drive the team back to town. His father's claim lay just southeast of Uncle John's, so the following day Sam came with Uncle John and the cousins to Edd's claim to help build a shanty.

Edd had spent the night wedged between two stacks of boards, rolled up in several blankets, with a layer of lumber

THE HOMESTEAD

between himself and the soggy ground. Although the Chinook had warmed the air during the day, the night was cold, and his body felt chilled and stiff by morning. When he rolled out of his blankets fully dressed, Edd had to stamp his feet and beat his hands together to warm them. After several brisk circuits of the pile of building materials, his eyes fell on the little iron stove he had purchased at the general store in Kenmare. The stove sat forlornly near the stacks of boards, a sack of coal leaning against it. Edd set about kindling a small fire in the iron box and soon he had water heating in his new coffee pot. By the time the other men arrived bearing several loaves of Aunt Mattie's fresh bread and a Dutch oven full of baked beans, Edd was warming his hands on a tin mug of coffee.

By nightfall the men had framed up a twelve-by-fourteen-foot shanty and a six-by-eight-foot shed for storing coal and grain. The shanty rested on wooden corner posts that raised the floor a foot off the ground. Its gable ends pointed north and south, and a boughten door opened in the south wall. A single, four-pane, casement window looked eastward. The granary sat at right angles to the shanty and was backed up closely against the shanty's north wall to form a windbreak. A door and window were cut into the granary's east wall and tightly lapped siding weatherproofed the building's exterior. The shanty's wide board walls were covered only by tarpaper secured by wooden battens, because Edd reasoned that with warmer weather on the way he could wait until fall, after his first crop of grain, to side the little house.

The next day, Edd finished the shanty's interior. He laid floorboards across the width of the house, set the little stove

IN THE HOLLOW OF GOD'S HAND

Edd's friends helped him build a twelve-foot by fourteen-foot claim shanty with a six-foot by eight-foot granary behind it for storing coal and grain.

in the middle of the west wall, and built a rough bunk in the northwest corner. Shelves behind the door held a few dishes and cooking pots; a packing crate at the end of the bed and several long nails protruding from the wall held clothing. Edd set a tiny drop-leaf table and two chairs in front of the window and the house was finished.

As the shanty neared completion, however, Edd noticed that he hadn't many nails left. So in the back corner of the house, beneath the bunk, he simply set floorboards on the joists without nailing them down.

"I'll get more nails the next time I'm in town," he said to

THE HOMESTEAD

himself, "and no one's going to walk on the floor under the bed anyway." But the next time he was in town he forgot to buy the nails, and soon he forgot all about the loose flooring.

The shanty was finished not a moment too soon: another spring snowstorm roared out of the northwest, and then another. The uninsulated shack was cold despite the red-hot stove. Wind gusted upward through cracks between the floorboards and fine ice crystals sifted in around the window and door. Between storms, Edd walked two miles south to the store at Baden to buy food supplies and order a delivery of coal. The Lundts had sold their store to Olaf Ribb and his sons, and Edd spent some time visiting with the Ribbs.

"How are you getting along out there on your claim?" Olaf asked.

"All right, I guess, but there's not much doing until spring plowing," Edd said. "I surely wouldn't mind a job somewhere."

"Well I hear the railroad might hire a few men to check the tracks," Olaf told him. "All this snow is slowing the trains down and they're worried that the river might flood when it melts."

Edd gave Olaf his full attention. "Who's doing the hiring?" he asked.

"I'd talk to Olsen, the station agent," Olaf suggested.

That was all the encouragement Edd needed to head for Kenmare.

CHAPTER 13: Stopping the Silk Train

"SURE, WE COULD USE ANOTHER MAN to trouble-check the tracks," Agent Olsen told Edd, "but you'd be working all hours of the day and night, and you'd need a good pocket watch. Are you living in town?" he asked.

"I'm homesteading a few miles south of town," Edd replied, "but I could board in town for a spell."

"Good, good," Olsen encouraged him. "Why don't you get settled and come back tomorrow morning and we'll put you to work."

Edd found a room in a boardinghouse and spent a few of his hard-earned dollars on a railroad pocket watch. The next day he reported for duty and was issued a train schedule and a lantern. The roundhouse foreman, Pete Waltz, showed Edd how to use the lantern to flag down a train at night if he found trouble on the tracks. Then Pete told him about rail traffic through the Des Lacs Valley.

"The Great Northern and Northern Pacific passenger trains mostly stop at Kenmare, 'though a few go on through to Minot," Pete said, "but they all slow down as they get close to town. Then there's the Soo Line freight trains and immigrant trains — a lot of them stop here, too. But it's the Great Northern and Milwaukee silk trains that 'r hardest to flag down when there's trouble; they don't stop for anything, and they run forty or more mile 'n hour." Pete shook his head. "They're afraid of bein' robbed, you see."

When Edd looked at him questioningly, Pete bit off a chaw of tobacco, offered the plug to Edd, then leaned back in his chair until it creaked in protest and related the history of the silk trains.

Although American colonists attempted silk production, or sericulture, as early as the 1700s, the labor-intensive process and its associated high costs soon encouraged the New World pioneers to leave sericulture to the Chinese. By the early 1900s, China was sending hundreds of tons of silk cocoons across the Pacific to feed the insatiable eastern mills of New York and New Jersey. Shiploads of the raw fibers regularly arrived at the West Coast ports of San Francisco; Seattle; and Vancouver, British Columbia, Pete said, where the cargo was loaded onto trains for its transcontinental journey. But not just any trains. The fastest engines the railroads could offer were pressed into service, along with special boxcars lined with burnished steel or varnished wood to minimize friction against the silk fibers. Speed was crucial, because a single shipment was worth two to four million dollars and the cocoons were perishable. When a China trader steamed into port in Vancouver, for example, dozens of the special baggage cars were shifted to that city, and once every twenty-four hours a trainload of silk sped eastward.

Those trains had the right of way, Pete said; dispatchers followed every mile of their progress and shunted freighters and passenger coaches onto sidings to let "the Silks" fly past. To

STOPPING THE SILK TRAIN

discourage robbers, silk trains carried armed guards and rarely stopped at public stations. What's more, they set speed records for coast-to-coast travel, arriving at their destinations only eighty to ninety hours after departure. When the engineer approached a town, he opened up the whistle and kept it blasting until the train, running at full steam, was a mile beyond the outskirts.

"So you see," Pete concluded, "stoppin' them trains is a tough job."

For the next month, Edd saddled a horse every morning and rode out along the tracks, northward or southward, to check for trouble. Each day the Des Lacs River was more swollen and the shallow lakes lapped farther outward as snow melted and ran off the slowly thawing ground. One afternoon a spring thunderstorm rolled up from the southwest, dropping its heavy load of moisture onto the already saturated prairie. Far north of town, Edd hunkered into his slicker and tried to calm his restive horse as the cold rain pummeled them.

When the deluge eased, Edd rode back towards Kenmare, watching the roiling dark clouds press down on the land as though night had fallen. Suddenly, up ahead, he saw the sheen of water: a long stretch of track lay submerged beneath the rising river. He reached under his slicker and his fingers probed for his watch — nearly four o'clock, and the daily silk train was due any moment. No time to walk through the rising water and check for a washout, he had to stop that train! He turned his horse and galloped northward for half a mile until he saw a stunted tree protruding from a depression in the land. Quickly he dismounted and tethered his horse securely to its twisted trunk, far enough from the tracks to prevent the animal from panicking when the train roared by.

He retrieved the signal lantern from his saddlebag, opened its curved metal door, and carefully lit the beeswax candle inside. Metal prongs secured the candle to the lantern's base and an inch-thick magnifying lens intensified the light a thousand-fold. When he was sure the candle was burning well, Edd rolled his matches up in their oilcloth pouch and tucked them into his pocket. As he withdrew his hand from beneath his slicker, he felt a slight vibration under his feet and heard the distant growl of the approaching freighter. He ran to the railbed, took a firm stand between the rails, and held the lantern aloft, moving it slowly back and forth as Pete had showed him.

Through the gathering darkness Edd saw the locomotive, still far away but coming on rapidly, its headlight piercing the gloom as it rushed toward him. He waved his signal lantern more vigorously and turned to step off the tracks, but as he did so he stumbled and the lantern flew out of his hand and rolled down the bank. Onward came the train and its roar seemed to fill his head. A surge of adrenalin raced through his body and, without being conscious of movement, he found himself at the bottom of the bank, fumbling with the lantern. He shoved his slicker aside and rammed his hand into his pocket, then swiftly unrolled the oiled packet of matches. The train's approaching rumble shook the earth as he crouched above the lantern, shielding the matches with his body. "One chance," he thought with cold clarity, "only one chance." He struck the match on the lantern's rough side and held it to the wick — it caught! — and he was up and running toward the tracks. Up went his arm, one sweep, two, and then the engine flew by him with a rush of air that almost knocked him backward. And still he swept his arm from side to side.

Seconds after he thought it was too late he heard the brakes shriek and grind, and all along the length of the iron horse sparks flew as its wheels locked and screamed against the rails. Edd began to run toward the engine, now far past him but slowing rapidly. When at last he reached it, the engine's front wheels had come to a stop only a few feet from the sheet of water that stretched before the train.

Two guards jumped down from the freight cars and approached Edd with rifles in hand, but when they saw the engine's headlight reflected on the widening spread of water their vigilance eased. They agreed that Edd should walk the tracks in front of the train to see whether it could safely continue. So foot by careful foot, his lantern held high, Edd examined the rails. The water was still shallow and had not deposited any debris on the tracks, so the train slowly followed him through the flooded area and continued on its way, bearing its costly burden of silk eastward.

Four more times that night Edd flagged down a train and walked it through the flood. Toward morning Pete sent someone to relieve him, and Edd gratefully rode back to his room at the boardinghouse where, after soaking the chill from his bones in a tin tub of steaming water, he slept through the day. By evening, the flood had begun to recede and the trains ran freely once again.

The Kenmare Hard Coal, Brick and Tile Company in Tasker's Coulee shipped four hundred tons of coal annually.

CHAPTER 14: Danger in the Mines

AFTER THE GROUND THAWED and dried, Edd plowed sod for his cousin Levi Kauffman, then borrowed Levi's oxen and turned over twenty-five acres of his own homestead. He didn't expect much of a harvest on newly broken ground, but he planted all twenty-five acres in oats. He also dug a well and planted ten trees. As he worked, Edd reflected on how far he'd come since striking out on his own four years previously. Besides the homestead, which he laughingly referred to as "the ranch," he had cash money in his pocket and an ever-growing circle of good friends.

He remembered again his boyhood in Ohio, and how the other children had shunned him when he came to school smelling of the musky fox, badger, and skunk he had trapped for their furs. Desperate to have something of his own in a family where he was largely ignored, Edd had sold or traded his furs at the general store for things he needed, such as schoolbooks or a pair of sturdy shoes.

One day when he was still very young, Edd bought a nickel's worth of penny candy and the storekeeper gave him change for his dime. Without looking at them, Edd slipped the five pennies into his pocket, where they jingled pleasantly during the long walk home. That night when he took off his overalls and put his pennies on the dresser, he found to his surprise that one of them was a rusty-looking discolored dime. Oh! He'd like to have kept it, but all night that dime lay heavily on his mind, and when he'd finished his chores the next morning he walked the long road to town to return it to the astonished tradesman.

"Well son," he remembered the storekeeper saying, "there's not many would have returned my money, nor walked so far to do it, so I believe we'll just split the difference." Whereupon the man handed Edd a nickel.

Edd also remembered his family's move to Missouri when he was eleven, right before the financial panic of 1893, and then their return to Ohio two years later after losing nearly everything they owned. Rather than discourage him, however, those tough times had birthed a determination to succeed in life and to act always with honesty and integrity.

Lying in bed in the warm summer nights, listening to the prairie winds sighing through the grasses, Edd tried to put his bitter childhood memories behind him and dream instead of finding a woman to share his life and give him children of his own. But he had little in the way of worldly goods, and he vowed that he would not marry until he could provide for a family. He could not know that six long years would pass before his dream was realized.

That fall, Edd worked in the harvest fields once again. When the settlers' grain was sacked and secure in their barns, he cast about for a winter job and soon found work as a coal miner.

In 1901 the Kenmare Hard Coal, Brick and Tile Company had established itself two miles southeast of Kenmare and began

DANGER IN THE MINES

The mine in winter: several boardinghouses in the coulee housed the miners.

pulling four hundred tons of soft coal from the earth annually. The company hired miners in the fall, after the harvest ended, and worked them until the demand for coal lessened in spring. For the next five years the cycle of spring and summer farm work, fall threshing, and winter mining provided stability and a steady income that allowed Edd to put down roots and to feel, at last, that he was a valued member of a community.

Nicknamed the Brickyard Mine, the colliery squatted in a bowl of land known as Tasker's Coulee. Gently sloping hills surrounded the buildings, sheltering them from the ever-present winds. The mineshaft cut deeply into a hill and spit forth a set of tracks that carried men into its depths and coal outward to the railroad

The brick works of the Kenmare Hard Coal, Brick and Tile Company, known locally as the Brickyard Mine, was prolific in output. The mine and brick works together employed fifteen to twenty-five men in summer and twice that many in winter.

siding, where it was loaded into freight cars. Two beehive-shaped buildings housed the brickworks, which fired twelve thousand pressed-clay rectangles a day, each brick proudly stamped KENMARE.

Scattered about the coulee, within an easy walk to mine and brick plant, were several homes and a boardinghouse run by the O'Neill family. North Dakota's harsh winter weather convinced most of the miners to live close to their work, and Edd was no exception. He camped in his claim shanty two days at the beginning and two days at end of each month to fulfill his homesteading requirements. The rest of the winter, Edd roomed at the boardinghouse and gratefully dined on Mrs. O'Neill's plain but hearty cooking.

DANGER IN THE MINES

Inside the Brickyard Mine, low-ceilinged shafts and rooms branched outward from the main alley. The soft coal ran in narrow seams through the rock and had to be blasted out with dynamite. The miners then shoveled the ore into wheeled trolleys that ran along tracks to the waiting rail cars outside the mine. As the lignite was blasted and dug out of the rock and earth, the miners constantly extended "rooms" of the mine into the hill. Timbers braced the walls and ceilings of those rooms, but occasionally the bracing failed and a cave-in occurred. Edd found that his every sense seemed heightened when he was underground, whether from fear or from a respect for elemental forces, he didn't know. At times, he imagined that he could feel faint tremors through the soles of his heavy work boots, or detect slight changes in the outward bulge of the rock and earthen walls.

One morning Edd felt increasingly uneasy as he worked, and several times he made excuse to go out to the mine's entrance. He was bracing a new shaft as the men cut deeper into the hill, and the roof seemed particularly unyielding as he pressed the beams into place. "I don't much like this hole," he told the man working next to him. "I just can't feel easy in my mind today."

Although the miners usually took their midday meal at one o'clock, often eating in the relative warmth underground, Edd talked the foreman into breaking a little early on the pretext of needing more timbers. Eager to leave the gloomy shaft, Edd strode quickly out into the bitingly cold fresh air and walked to the boardinghouse for lunch. Sitting at the dining table, his uneasiness abated, but even as he raised a spoonful of boiled beef and cabbage to his mouth he heard the mine whistle shriek the sustained blast that meant *cave in*.

The men shoved their chairs back from the table and rushed across the yard to the mine, which belched a gaseous cloud of coal dust. The foreman vouched for the fact that no one was underground — all the men were accounted for — so uneasily the miners returned to their noon meal, awaiting word as to when they could go back to work. The next morning Foreman Drake gave the okay and the men straggled back down the shaft, some with obvious reluctance, others with joking bravado. But Edd entered the mine calmly and returned to the room where he had been working, only to find that the entire roof had collapsed.

From then on, the other miners watched Edd closely, some with an almost superstitious caution, for the man working next to him had told the others about Edd's premonition. Now, when Edd insisted that a tunnel needed more bracing, the men worked with a will. But one day even Edd's intuition couldn't save him entirely. Picking away in an alley he suddenly felt dizzy. He stood up sharply and swung around toward the entrance, but his legs seemed made of rubber. "Everyone out," he yelled, "gas in the mine!" He tried desperately to move forward, but the ground rushed up to meet him and blackness rolled over him.

When he regained consciousness, Edd lay in the snow near the mine's entrance, gasping for breath. Someone had risked his own life to drag Edd out after he collapsed. Several miners sat nearby, heads resting on their hands or leaning back against the coal cars.

"Hurry, get these men into the wagon," the foreman hollered, and Edd felt himself lifted onto a pallet and jostled from side to side as the wagon rolled over the frozen ground. He drifted in and out of blackness on the two-mile trip to town and was only half aware of being carried into the hospital and stretched out on a clean white bed, coal-dust-covered clothing and all.

When he awoke the next morning, he remembered being violently ill during the night and the sensation of smooth, cool hands holding his head over a basin as he retched. At that moment, a motherly looking woman dressed in starched white cloth bustled into Edd's room, followed closely by a dapper young man wearing a concerned expression.

"How are you feeling, Mr. Yoder?" the doctor inquired. "It's a miracle you're still with us; you got quite a dose of that mine gas, you know." The doctor checked Edd over thoroughly and told him he must stay quietly in the hospital for several days until all the gas was out of his blood.

"You must be able to eat without nausea and not feel any dizziness at all before we can release you," the doctor prescribed, and as he turned to leave Edd heard him mutter to himself, "Lucky man, very lucky indeed."

Unlike his ordeal in the lumber camp pest house, Edd's brief stay in the Kenmare hospital was almost pleasant. The nurses vied for the job of caring for the handsome, soft-spoken young man, and Edd teased and flirted with the younger ones, who always left his room smiling. When he was released, he rested for a few days at the boardinghouse, where Mrs. O'Neill fussed over him and fed him well. Before long he was back in the mine, earning his twenty dollars a week — a sum that was soon to make him the focus of unwelcome attention.

CHAPTER 15: Thieves in the Night

DESPITE ITS MOSTLY LAW-ABIDING citizens and able sheriff, Kenmare was still a rough-and-ready western frontier town. Cattle rustlers, horse thieves, and gangs of cutthroats roamed the countryside, and desperation sometimes drove even law-abiding citizens to crime.

Edd moved back to his claim when the weather warmed, but he continued to work at the Brickyard Mine until planting season. He didn't mind walking the mile and a half to work along the railroad tracks, even though it meant going home after dark. The last Friday in April was payday and the miners were always paid in cash. Edd picked up his pay as usual and started for home. Although he had an account at the First National Bank of Kenmare, it was too late in the evening to deposit his money. He'd ride into town with a neighbor later on, he decided.

Edd was striding down the rail spur toward the main track when he heard running footsteps coming up behind him. He turned to see who it was and nearly collided with young Ben O'Neill.

"What's your hurry, Ben?" Edd asked the fifteen-year-old boy.

"I heard one of the men at the mine talking with a stranger, Edd," Ben gasped, as he tried to catch his breath. "They were talking about you, and how you walked home along the tracks to your claim and —" Ben looked worried. "Well, it sounded like they were planning to follow you tonight. I thought you should know," he finished.

Edd thought for a moment, then he said, "Thank you for warning me, Ben. You go on back to the boardinghouse now," he continued, "but cut across the prairie so no one sees you. I'll be all right, now that I know to keep an eye out."

Ben lost no time in disappearing into the darkness, and Edd let him get a good start before he turned southwest, away from the railroad, and set a brisk pace across the fields. When he came to the road that marked the quarter section, he kept it on his right, but continued treading through the wheat stubble. The moon climbed steadily above the horizon and countless stars glowed from a clear sky, so Edd had no fear of losing his way. If I see anyone in the distance, I can lie down in the stubble and wait until they pass by, he thought.

When he judged that he'd walked as far south as his homestead, which sat in the middle of a section, he turned east, and soon saw the buildings looming before him. He approached the shanty cautiously, but everything looked to be in order. Edd unlocked the front door and reached for the kerosene lantern, which hung on a peg just inside the door. He lit the wick and replaced the glass chimney, then stepped inside the shanty and closed the door behind him with a relieved sigh.

His relief was short-lived, however — a brown-coated shape sprang from the bed and slunk behind the stove, growling deep in its throat, its shadow looming halfway up the wall in the lantern light. Edd yelled with surprise and, still grasping the lantern, jumped toward the back corner of the house. Just as quickly the coyote — for that's what it was, Edd saw — ran for the door, which unfortunately was closed. Around the room they went, Edd making a move, then the coyote, then Edd again, until, reaching the door at last, Edd flung it open and leaped away, whereupon the animal snarled and sped through the opening to freedom.

Drenched with sweat and breathing heavily, Edd carefully set the lantern down and sank onto the bed, when suddenly his eyes fell on the smoked bacon he had hung from the ceiling to keep it safe from mice. "Well that's what the coyote was after," Edd muttered, "but how —?" He stood up and looked around the room, but no obvious means of ingress could be seen. Puzzled, he turned in a full circle, surveying walls, roof, and floor, when all at once he spied several tufts of gray-brown fur snagged on a floorboard beneath the bed. Kneeling down, he saw that one of the wide boards was askew, and all at once he remembered the shortage of nails when he was building the shanty and the unsecured flooring beneath the bunk. Pleased that he had solved the mystery, Edd reached for his heavy Dutch oven and placed it atop the boards to weight them down until morning.

"Tomorrow I'll make a trip to town if I have to walk all the way there and back," he vowed. "I'll put my money in the bank and buy some nails and *finish that floor!*"

Alice Troyer's friends Anna Harshbarger, left, and Agnes Andrews stand outside the cook car where Alice cooked for the North Dakota threshing crew.

CHAPTER 16: Threshing

SOUTHWESTERN WINDS RIPPLED THROUGH luxuriant fields of wheat, oats, corn, and rye as the grains ripened steadily beneath the blazing Dakota sun. Cool rains had watered the crops early in the season and a bumper harvest seemed assured, Edd thought, eyeing the fields authoritatively. Now twenty-seven years old, Edd had prospered during his years on the prairie. His homestead claim boasted thirty-nine acres under cultivation, and he had purchased and planted an additional eighty acres from neighbor George Frost when George's advanced years made farming difficult. Edd's perseverance and frugal lifestyle had yielded both a healthy bank account and money loaned out at interest to friends. He still lived simply, but when the occasion demanded Edd wore tailored suits, the finest shoes, and a silk tie secured by an ornate stickpin.

Although he worked hard, Edd played just as hard. His crowd of intimates was a lighthearted gang that knew how to have fun. The group included Fred Friis, vice-president of Kenmare's only bank, and up-and-coming homesteaders Coy Collins, Sam Galyen, Dan Miller, and Will Yoder. They squired Kenmare's most attractive young women to Chautauquas — where Edd frequently won the prize for best oration — spelling bees, boating excursions, the annual Fourth of July celebration along the Mouse River, and Sunday evening social events held at private homes or in one of Kenmare's many churches. Edd's reputation as a jokester and a spellbinding storyteller ensured his popularity with men and women alike, but try as they might, his female companions made little headway in capturing his heart. Always gallant, always willing to show a girl a good time, Edd avoided pairing off permanently with any of the young women in his circle of friends.

In that summer of 1908, Lee Kauffman also kept a close eye on the crops as they matured, gauging the likelihood of a successful harvest. In addition to his own two hundred acres, Lee also carried the burden of his father's one hundred and sixty acres: Uncle John had died three years ago, leaving a daughter and two sons still at home with Aunt Mattie. So when the weather remained gentle and predictable and the grain grew tall and full in the husk, Lee gambled: he leased threshing equipment and asked Edd to head up a crew. Edd was happy to do it. After six years as one of the threshers, he was gratified to be the boss.

Lee also bought a railroad boxcar that had been converted to a rough field kitchen. Horses pulled the cook car from farm to farm so that the threshers could have hearty, hot meals to begin and end their workdays. Lee hired two young women to do the cooking: Anna Harshbarger, who lived in the Mennonite community at Baden, and Alice Troyer, who was visiting from Oregon.

The railroads' increasing reach had made it possible for Mennonites from communities in Oregon, Idaho, the Dakotas,

THRESHING

Edd Yoder's threshing crew cutting grain on the North Dakota prairie.

Missouri, Ohio, and Pennsylvania to visit back and forth with some frequency. Winter months, when farming chores were few, were especially popular for visiting, but young men and women often spent an entire summer or winter living far from home. Several young people from North Dakota had sojourned in Oregon the previous winter and one of them, Agnes Andrews, had become good friends with Alice Troyer.

An adventurous twenty-year-old, Alice had already lived away from home while working at a bakery in the bustling metropolis of Portland, a day's wagon ride from her parents' farm. Eager to see more of the world, Alice decided to accompany Agnes and the others when they returned to North Dakota in May. The women stopped to visit relatives in the Mennonite community in Nampa, Idaho, then continued eastward to arrive at Baden in midsummer. Word of Alice's cooking and baking skills soon spread throughout the community, and Lee lost no time in offering her the position of head cook for the threshing crew.

Hustling up three meals a day in the cramped cook car for a large group of hungry men was a daunting task. At five o'clock each morning, Alice began mixing dough for twelve loaves of bread while Anna Harshbarger griddled stacks of pancakes and brewed a large pot of coffee. While the bread dough was rising, Alice fried potatoes or rashers of bacon and several dozen eggs, then the women dished up breakfast. After breakfast, as soon as the bread came out of the oven, Alice put meat to roast in the wood burning cookstove while the women washed dishes and began preparing the next meal.

If the men were coming in from the fields at noon, Anna and Alice spent the morning peeling potatoes and preparing vegetables. More often, they made dishpans full of sandwiches and gallons of cold tea and took those, along with pies, cakes, and cookies, out to the threshers. Then the men sat down to a hot evening meal at the cook car. Afternoons, or sometimes after supper, Alice stewed dried fruit and baked the cakes and pies the crew would eat the following day, while Anna washed dishes or chased down and butchered several chickens. Finally, when the baking, meal planning, and preparations for the next day were complete and Anna had gone home, Alice walked or rode to Mattie Kauffman's farmhouse and dropped exhaustedly into bed.

When his cousin Lee introduced him to the capable young woman from Oregon, Edd was impressed by Alice's vivacious manner and ready laugh. The tall girl with warm brown eyes, a generous

THRESHING

mouth, and a wealth of auburn hair made a jolly addition to the community. And could she ever cook! Edd savored the sweet, rich pies and meltingly tender applesauce cakes she baked and admired her finely roasted meats and fluffy mashed potatoes swimming in gravy.

Sometimes Anna prepared the evening meal, but her repertoire consisted mainly of vegetable soup — with heavy emphasis on turnips and potatoes. The men joked about that soup at first, but by the end of the season a groan often met the news that it was Anna's turn to cook. Moreover, Anna and crewmember Levi Yoder were sparking, and they made no secret of their mutual attraction. Anna flirted and giggled as she served the food, but if Levi attended to his meal too assiduously she pouted until he paid her some attention.

Alice had a serious beau in Oregon, so although she was friendly with all the men, she declined to flirt. The more she saw of Edd, however, the more she respected his quiet authority with the other men. His strong, square-jawed face and deep-set, flashing blue eyes, a well-shaped mouth that was quick to smile or make a joke, and the dark blond hair that waved back from a broad forehead were certainly handsome, Alice thought. And he worked hardest of all the crew; he was the first man in the field in the morning and the last to sit down to supper at night. He often looked so exhausted that Alice began to think of little things she might do to ease the burden of his responsibility.

One evening after the threshers had washed up and seated themselves at the long trestle table, Edd walked in from the field, hot, dirty, and tired, carrying a broken piece of machinery. As

Anna continued to serve the food, Alice quickly emptied and refilled a washbasin and laid a clean towel next to it, then continued bringing out bowls of potatoes and vegetables and platters of fried prairie chicken and bread. Edd leaned for a moment against the side of the cook car. Then he bent over, plunged his arms into the basin, and splashed water on his face. Abruptly he stopped. The water was warm! Expecting to feel cold well water that scarcely lathered the stinging lye soap, he didn't know what to make of the soothing sensation of warm water against his dust-covered skin. He washed slowly and thoroughly, savoring the luxury, then gratefully dried his sunburned face and arms on the soft, clean towel. As he took his place at the table, Edd flashed Alice a grateful smile, which she acknowledged with a smile of her own. From then on, Alice always brought him a basin of fresh water after the other men finished their ablutions, and the water was always warm.

After supper, Edd saddled a horse and rode to Kenmare to replace a broken separator part. He rousted the storekeeper out of bed to open the store and it was nearly midnight by the time they completed their business. Edd stabled his horse at the livery barn and flopped down in the sweet-smelling hay in an empty stall to catch a few hours of sleep. Then, well before dawn, he rode back to the harvest field. As he came abreast of the cook car he saw that its lanterns were lit; Alice was starting her early morning bread making. She heard the horse's hooves thudding against the parched ground and called through the open door.

"Good morning, Edd. You've put in a long night. Will you stop in for a moment?"

THRESHING

"Good morning, Alice," Edd replied. He dismounted and looped the horse's reins over the stair rail, then sat down on the top step, almost too tired to speak.

"Here's a little something to keep you until breakfast," Alice said, handing him a tall glass of milk saved from her baking and a tin plate holding a large slice of dried peach pie. Edd took a swallow of the fresh milk and it tasted so good he drank nearly the entire glass before he set it down and tucked into the pie. When he had scooped up every last sugary crumb and drained every drop of milk from the glass, Edd stood up, stretched, and sighed deeply.

"That puts heart into a man," he said gratefully, thinking of her kindness as much as the food. "Thank you, Allie."

"You are most welcome," she said, smiling softly.

She was still smiling as Edd rode off to repair the grain separator before breakfast.

A steam engine drives the thresher, or separator, which separates grain from straw.

CHAPTER 17: New Friends

BLACK SMOKE POURED from the steam engine's stovepipe, guiding Alice and Anna to the threshing site. When the women reached the busy scene, Anna reined in the horses and she and Alice sat on the wagon seat watching the men work.

A yards-long, heavy woven belt rotated tautly between the clanking, coal-fired steam engine and the gears of the threshing machine, or separator. Edd stood in front of the separator feeder, pitching bundles of wheat headfirst into its grinding maw. He pivoted his upper body and caught a heavy bundle tossed to him butt-first by the wagon driver, who stood atop a load of sheaves, then used the momentum of the catch to swing his body around in a smooth motion, releasing the sheaf as it came abreast of the feeder. The feeder's teeth chopped grain from straw and blew the wheat kernels out one chute while it ground the remaining straw into short pieces and blew them out another chute.

Most of the grain was poured directly into wagons for transshipment to Minnesota's flour mills, but some was shoveled into burlap sacks for seed wheat or to be milled into flour at the Danish-built windmill north of Kenmare. Horse teams hauled wagon after wagon piled high with sheaves in from the fields as other teams took the threshed grain away.

Ernest Squire, the tank man, drew his horse drawn water wagon alongside the steam engine. He jumped to the ground and swiftly hooked up a hose, then hand pumped vigorously to transfer water into the steam engine's holding tank. Meanwhile, the stoker kept the machine's firebox filled with coal.

As Alice watched the hum of activity, Edd noticed that the women had arrived and his voice rang out in a prearranged signal to halt the threshing. The wagon man completed his toss and, as agreed, sent one final bundle of wheat flying toward Edd, who flung it into the feeder and motioned to Ernest, who opened the valve that released the boiler's steam pressure. Abruptly, the clanking machinery slowed and stopped. Edd stretched the kinks from his arms and shoulders and jumped to the ground as the women began unloading food for the noon meal.

The threshers quickly consumed hearty slabs of roast beef and layers of cold baked beans sandwiched between thick slices of homemade bread, and they peeled and ate cold boiled potatoes sprinkled with salt. Alice also set out kettles of raw onion rings in vinegar and bowls of sliced raw turnips. Then she uncovered a dishpan heaped with half-moon pies, a traditional Amish–Mennonite turnover filled with cooked dried apples sweetened with brown sugar and flavored with cinnamon. Half-moon pies were a favorite of Edd's, and he ate several of the sugary treats as his friend Ernest teased him about his good appetite.

Alice also handed Edd a small jug of cold milk to wash down his lunch.

"Say, how come he always gets somethin' special?" Ernest objected, half-teasing, half-serious. "That's not fair!"

NEW FRIENDS

Harvesting grain in North Dakota.

"But look how hard he works," Alice replied, so softly that only Ernest could hear her. And Ernest grudgingly admitted that it was so.

One Sunday, Alice joined Anna's family for services at the Spring Valley Mennonite Church near Baden, then went home with them for dinner. At church, Alice found herself looking to see whether Edd was there, and she was surprisingly disappointed that he wasn't. But later that afternoon, as she sat outdoors on a quilt with her back against the house enjoying the late summer sunshine, Alice saw a buggy spinning down the road, trailing a dust cloud. Drowsily, she shaded her eyes with her hand, then sat up and smoothed her windblown hair as Edd drove up to the house and halted the team with a flourish.

"Miss Alice," he said, doffing his smooth, narrow-brimmed black hat with a mischievous grin, "could I interest you in a buggy ride?"

Alice grinned back, drowsiness forgotten, her cheeks reddened from more than sun and prairie wind. "Why yes," she replied, "I would like that. But I was planning to go to the young people's meeting at church this evening with Anna and Levi. Would you like to have an early supper with us and then go to the meeting?"

Edd didn't hesitate. "That sounds like fun," he said, "if you're sure it's no trouble for me to stay to supper."

While Edd watered and secured the horses, Alice flew into the house and combed her hair, then tied on an apron and helped Anna's mother set out a cold repast of home cured ham and potato salad. Anna had been out buggy riding with Levi, but they returned in time to sit down to the meal with the rest of the family. Afterwards, Mrs. Harshbarger shooed the young people out the door, insisting that she and Anna's younger sisters would take care of the kitchen chores. In truth, the mother was eager to see Anna married, for the Harshbarger's many children were a heavy drain on the family's meager resources — hence Anna's expertise with the recipe for vegetable soup.

Edd helped Alice into his rented buggy, then set out a little way behind Levi and Anna. By the time they all arrived at the church, the meeting had begun. Harmonious *a capella* singing swelled from the open windows as the men tied their horses to the hitching rail and the women smoothed their hair and skirts. The song ended and a man began speaking as Edd and Alice led the way into the church. The speaker glanced up at the two

NEW FRIENDS

couples, then stopped midsentence as he saw Alice's hand resting in the curve of Edd's arm. As one, the seated men and women turned to look in a suddenly deafening silence as the latecomers took their seats. Alice heard a sibilant indrawn breath followed by a female voice speaking just loudly enough to carry to the back of the tiny church.

"Huh!" the voice said. "If that missy from Oregon thinks she's going to catch Edd Yoder, she's got another think coming!"

The girl's seatmate jabbed an elbow into her side and she huffily faced frontward again. Levi cleared his throat noisily and shuffled his feet to drown out any further comments, and the young man behind the pulpit recollected himself and abashedly continued his remarks.

Astonished, but coolly in control of her dignity, Alice ignored the stares and the rude outburst. When another hymn swelled forth, she harmonized her full-throated alto to Edd's soprano and thoroughly enjoyed herself, music being her greatest delight.

When the service ended, Edd lost no time in shepherding Alice outdoors into the crisp evening air, and his buggy was the first to leave the churchyard. The starry, moonlit night demanded appreciation, so he turned the well-rested horses toward the open prairie and let them have their heads. The lovely night sky made Alice feel like singing, and sing she did, one hymn after another, as Edd listened appreciatively and kept the horses at a smooth trot. Soon they reached the shore of Lower Des Lacs Lake, where Edd reined the team to a slow walk along the moon-dappled water. Superb raconteur that he was, Edd soon had Alice laughing helplessly at his humorous tales of homesteading life.

"Seven brothers came to North Dakota and took a one-hundred-sixty-acre claim," Edd began his story. "Poor as church mice, the brothers had only enough money to build a one-room shanty, so they constructed a shelf six feet wide across one end of the crude building and at night they all piled onto the shelf to sleep. The seven strapping men filled that bed from wall to wall, packed in like herrings in a can, and not a one could turn over unless they all did, which meant that they had to wake each other up each time they wanted to change position, and that made them all cross.

"The oldest brother scratched his head over the problem and finally lit on a solution. Any brother who wanted to turn over would holler out 'spoon,' and the rest of the brothers would all turn together. The eldest figured that soon the brothers would get to where they could turn over practically in their sleep and, sure enough, they all learned to roll over reflexively whenever they heard the word 'spoon.'

"One summer Sunday, I and a group of my friends, including three of the brothers, spent the day swimming and picnicking by the Des Lacs River. As the afternoon wore on, several of the men grew sleepy and stretched out to nap on a narrow log footbridge that spanned the river. As Otis Ogburn and I sat on the bank talking, Otis nudged me and suggested, 'Let's holler *spoon* and see what happens to those sleepyheads.' On the count of three, we yelled in unison and watched gleefully as all three brothers rolled off the bridge and into the river with a mighty splash."

Alice laughed heartily at Edd's stories, and she was still chuckling when the buggy rolled into the Kauffman's farmyard.

NEW FRIENDS

As she bid Edd goodnight and slipped into the house, she decided that she'd seldom had so much fun, despite her chilly reception at the young people's meeting and the jealous comment she had overheard. A little guiltily, Alice thought of Frank Zook, her beau back home, but Oregon and Frank seemed very far away, and she dismissed the thought and went, smiling, to bed.

Nov. 27, 1908.   DND   02017
                                                                11.8300
                              4—196.
Final Certificate No. ....   Application No. 18974

HOMESTEAD.

Department of the Interior,

UNITED STATES LAND OFFICE,

Minot, North Dakota
NOV 27, 1908
...., 190....

It is hereby certified That, pursuant to the provisions of Section No. 2291, Revised Statutes of the United States, Edward Yoder has made payment in full for SW¼NE¼

of Section No. 9, in Township No. 159, of Range No. 88, of the 5th Principal Meridian west, containing 40 acres.

Now, therefore, be it known, That on presentation of this certificate to the COMMISSIONER OF THE GENERAL LAND OFFICE, the said Edward Yoder shall be entitled to a patent for the tract of land above described

                                    [signature]
                                              Register.
18974 Kenmare.   0-4

02017

Edd Yoder proved up on his North Dakota homestead in fall 1908, winning his bet with the U.S. government that he could occupy and cultivate the land for five years.

CHAPTER 18: A Parting of the Ways

ALICE HEARD A WAGON CLATTER to a halt outside the cook car. She poked her head out the door to see who could be arriving in midafternoon and gasped as she saw Edd prostrate atop bundles of wheat in the wagon bed, his face pale beneath his tan. Ernest jumped down from the wagon seat.

"Horse kicked him in the leg," Ernest said economically, "I'm haulin' him into town, but we could use a jug o' water to take along."

"Of course, I'll just be a minute," Alice said, as she ducked back inside. In moments she was back with a crockery jug of water plus two tin cups of hot coffee and several bread and butter sandwiches. After she handed everything to the men, she reached into her apron pocket and retrieved a small bottle of liniment she had brought with her from Oregon.

"Would you like me to take a look at your leg before you go?" she asked Edd.

Lips pressed tightly together against the pain, Edd nodded, and Alice climbed up into the wagon box while he pushed himself upright and rolled up his trousers. Edd's right leg was swollen and a large purplish lump had formed near his knee. Alice lost no time in applying liniment, but gentle as she was, Edd winced as her fingers lightly massaged his knee and calf. When she finished, she wiped her hands on her apron and handed him the bottle.

"Keep this as long as it helps you," she told Edd, then said to Ernest, "if you can't find the doctor right away, try to get some ice for the swelling."

Ernest finished his coffee and handed Alice his empty cup, tipped his hat, slapped the reins over the horses' backs, and the wagon rolled toward Kenmare.

The next morning Edd hobbled to breakfast on one leg, a stout stick serving as a crutch. He thanked Alice for her solicitous care the day before, particularly for the liniment, which he said had begun to ease the pain immediately. "Doc says he doesn't think anything's broken, but he wants me to put as little weight on the leg as possible for a week or so," Edd said. "Of course, I have to keep threshing."

Alice shook her head at that, but said only, "I'm relieved that your injury isn't more serious." Nevertheless, she redoubled her efforts to ensure that Edd had as many small comforts as she could provide. Edd made a comical sight as he hobbled about with his stick and the men teased him considerably, but within a week he was able to walk unsupported. When he returned the remaining liniment to Alice, he accompanied it with another heartfelt "thank you" and a little red-and-white-striped paper bag full of candy from town.

The men finished threshing in mid-October. Her job completed, Alice prepared to leave North Dakota before winter weather made travel difficult. She decided to visit relatives in Garden

A PARTING OF THE WAYS

City, Missouri, for a few months before returning to Oregon. Edd was leaving Dakota for the winter, too. After five years of homesteading, he would prove up his claim in November and then he would be free to travel.

The previous winter Edd had spent three months in Ohio, seeing his family again after five long years away. Most of his stepbrothers and stepsisters were young adults now, although he had two little sisters he scarcely knew: they had been two and five years old when he left Ohio in 1902. Edd was surprised at how good it felt to be with his family again. Much of the resentment he carried with him when he left Ohio had melted away during his years on the prairie. Also, as he matured into manhood, Edd had learned more about the complexities of human nature, and he now understood that people of worth existed side by side with hypocrites in every community and every religious practice.

Since the Sunday evening when he escorted Alice to the young people's meeting, Edd had spent several weekend evenings visiting with her at the Kauffmans'. Aunt Mattie rigorously played chaperone, ensuring that their lighthearted tête-á-têtes lasted for only an hour before she joined them and kept them company for the rest of the evening. On the Sunday before Alice left Dakota, Edd concluded his evening visit by asking whether he could write to her and if she would write back.

"You have been a kind friend to me, Allie," he said soberly. "I will miss you."

Alice left the Kauffman farm shortly after sunrise on a frosty, late-October morning. Until the moment she climbed into the spring wagon for the trip to Kenmare to catch the train, she secretly harbored the hope that Edd would stop by the cook car to say goodbye. Anna was keeping the kitchen open for a few more days while a skeleton crew performed maintenance on the threshing machinery, and Alice helped Anna prepare breakfast one last time. But Edd failed to appear.

The eastern sky flamed red as the sun swung above the horizon, warming the frosty air only slightly. As the wagon jolted toward Kenmare, Alice surveyed the mellow grasslands in their golden, year-end splendor and decided that she would very much like to return. Something about this place had captured her heart, although she wasn't quite sure what that something was. But the lonely calls of Canada geese as they winged north in strict formation reinforced an empty feeling she couldn't altogether blame on her scanty breakfast.

On the last day of October, Edd found a letter waiting for him in the postal drop at the Baden store. Alice wrote that she had arrived safely in Missouri in time to see her parents, who were visiting there, too, but that she didn't much care for "Mo." She enquired when Edd was leaving for Ohio and suggested that she might travel East herself in a month or two.

Edd planned to stay in North Dakota through November; his homestead would be proved up on the twenty-fourth. Until then, he and Chester Hartzler — brother of Charles Hartzler, who had married Edd's sister Lydia — were baching it in the claim shanty. Edd urged Alice to travel East, perhaps accompanying his Aunt Mattie and Cousin Willie, who planned to spend the winter

A PARTING OF THE WAYS

visiting relatives in Missouri and Ohio. Edd also encouraged her to return to North Dakota in the fall to cook for the threshers, perhaps with her good friend Agnes.

A faithful flow of letters now commenced, and soon each of the writers looked eagerly for his or her weekly letter. The letters told of little beyond news of people they knew and the pulse of daily activities, although Edd's never failed to reminisce about jokes they had shared during the harvest — particularly Anna's penchant for serving vegetable "Suppe." Nevertheless, between the laconically written lines, affection continued to grow.

To gain his property deed from the government, Edd was required to place a weekly notice in the *Kenmare Journal* for six weeks prior to making final five-year proof, thus allowing any challengers to come forward. Edd paid the publication and notary fees of six dollars and seventy-five cents and the notice was duly posted. Additionally, four witnesses were required to sign an affidavit, and two witnesses must give oral testimony supporting Edd's contention that he had made the required improvements to the land. Laurits Rytter, Frank Engels, A.J. Hooks, and Ernest Squire — all neighbors and friends — signed the affidavit, and Laurits and Frank traveled with Edd to the U.S. Land Office at Minot to testify. After paying a final recording fee of two dollars and twenty-five cents, Edd jubilantly received his patent to the forty acres, which were valued at approximately five hundred dollars.

Enormously relieved and eager to enjoy some of the fruits of his years of labor, Edd looked forward to a pleasant winter of relaxation, interspersed with visits to relatives in several states.

His joy spilled over in his letters to Alice; he joked and teased with lighthearted abandon, and she — now quite enjoying herself in Missouri — answered his letters in kind. But the winter was to bring new tests of Edd's maturity and lead him in an unexpected direction.

A fierce Dakota blizzard roared out of the north on November 30, mounding snow high against the shanty's walls. Edd and Chester huddled near the glowing stove during the day and burrowed deeply into woolen blankets heaped on the bunks at night. By morning, the storm had blown itself out, and the men peered out the window at once-familiar landscape features now obscured by drifted snow.

"I guess that's my cue to head home to Missouri," Chester said, laughing. And without further delay he began packing his trunk. The next day Edd borrowed Lee's wagon and drove Chester and his brother, Oliver, who had been working at the Kauffman's farm, to the station at Kenmare. Then he was alone once more.

There's always a jolly nice crowd that comes up here in the fall, and then they leave one by one until they are all gone, Edd wrote to Alice. *I am glad that I am one of them that's going this fall. I don't know when I will come back.*

Within the week, Edd boarded a train to Ohio.

CHAPTER 19: Courting

THE HOLIDAYS USHERED IN a whirlwind of social activity to West Liberty, Ohio. Aunt Mattie and Cousin Willie arrived from Dakota, and Edd accompanied them in round after round of visiting during the two weeks before Christmas. He also attended a church conference, greeting old friends and making several new ones.

Christmas dinner around the big table at Yoders' brought reminiscences of other times together and of family members, such as Uncle John, who were no longer with them. Through it all, Edd enjoyed his status as adult son and elder brother — and a materially successful one at that — wearing his handsome suits with ease and regaling the family with his pioneering tales.

But in the New Year, tragedy struck. Sister Ola Mae fell ill after spending the night with her best friend, Anna King. Within days, Ola Mae — along with Anna and Anna's younger sister and two brothers — was diagnosed with deadly typhoid fever. The typhoid spread quickly through West Liberty. Townspeople and country dwellers alike sequestered themselves in their homes, suspending all visiting until the fever ran its course. Sadly, in the depths of a bitterly cold January, Ola Mae's friend Anna King died.

Somehow it fell to Edd to take care of his sister. *Mother isn't well and it seems there is so much work for the rest to do*, he wrote to Alice. For many days Edd feared for Ola Mae's life. Night after night he sat by her bed as fever consumed her body and she cried out in delirium, and his own strength was nearly at an end when Aunt Mattie returned from a sojourn in Bellfontaine and relieved him of full-time nursing.

Under Aunt Mattie's skillful care, Ola Mae began a slow journey to recovery, but February had nearly passed before she was able to leave her bed. The brother and sister had planned to visit relatives and friends together and Edd chafed at his long restriction indoors, but it could not be helped.

As winter wearily advanced, Edd's eighty-three-year-old Grandpa Yoder gradually succumbed to old age and poor health. The failing patriarch needed constant care, so Edd's father, Ezra, and Uncle Dave took turns sitting up with the old man at night. When February rolled into March and Ola Mae's recovery seemed assured, Edd was pressed into service to help care for his grandfather.

Edd intended to travel to Missouri toward the end of March to visit his sister Lydia, and he hoped to see Alice as well. Their weekly letters had included an exchange of photographs, and Alice had invited Edd to travel West with her and several other Mennonite young people. But when Grandpa Yoder's condition worsened, Edd began to doubt that he would arrive in Missouri before Alice returned to Oregon for her sister Ida's wedding. As much as Alice wanted to be at the wedding, however, she longed to see Edd even more, so she continued to delay her departure.

COURTING

Winter increasingly clutched old Daniel Yoder in its frigid grasp, and on March 19 he drew his last breath. His funeral attracted one of the largest crowds the county had witnessed. Daniel's seven children, including Aunt Fannie — now married to Paul Whitmere of Goshen, Indiana; twenty-four grandchildren; and many friends and neighbors came to pay their last respects. After the service, Aunt Fannie extracted a firm promise from Edd to visit them in Goshen on his way to Missouri, thus delaying his arrival in the West even more.

Edd found that he was more than ready to leave Ohio. Without further delay he boarded a train: traveling first to Indiana, then to Michigan to spend a few precious days with his stepbrother Dan, and at last to Missouri. Seven and a half years would pass before he would see his birthplace in Ohio again and, when he did, his life would have drastically changed.

If nothing prevents, I will be in Missouri the last of this week, Edd wrote Alice. *I will likely get to see you at Garden City on Saturday afternoon, or at church Sunday. I would enjoy your company Sunday very much if it suits you. Please drop me a line and tell me where you will be, and I could make arrangements for a rig.*

Alice's heartbeat quickened as she read Edd's brief note, mailed from a train station enroute to Missouri. He would arrive, perhaps, tomorrow! What would it be like to see him again after five months and so many letters? She immediately sat down at the parlor desk and wrote a reply, which she sent by messenger to the Hartzlers, where Edd would be staying with his sister Lydia.

IN THE HOLLOW OF GOD'S HAND

I would be pleased to see you on Saturday afternoon, or to accompany you to church on Sunday. At present, I am staying with my Aunt Mattie Troyer. You are welcome to drop in any time.

On the second Friday in April, Edd arrived in Garden City and his brother-in-law, Charley Hartzler, met him at the station. Lydia was at home caring for their four children, Charley explained, including their four-month-old baby boy. When at last they reached the Hartzler home, Lydia's gentle smile told Edd that she was very glad to see her little brother. "And you have a letter waiting for you," she said mischievously.

Without looking to see who had sent it, Edd took the letter and nonchalantly tucked it into his pocket. As soon as he was alone, however, he read the missive eagerly and smiled at its contents.

I've never met a woman I thought so much of, not even my sisters, he admitted to himself. *But perhaps she doesn't think as much of me as I do of her.* He frowned anxiously, then his expression cleared. *Guess I'll find out how she feels tomorrow!* he concluded.

Alice stood up swiftly when she heard Edd's firm knock on the front door Saturday afternoon, but she waited patiently as her aunt opened the door and ushered the guest into the parlor. And suddenly, there he was, as tall as she remembered and even more good looking, grinning broadly at seeing her again. Alice felt strangely calm as she put her hand out to meet his, and as Edd wrapped his calloused brown fingers around her capable but soft ones they both experienced the curious sensation that they had known each other forever, and as no one else ever could.

COURTING

Aunt Mattie left them alone then, and they visited about inconsequential things, neither giving the social chatter their full attention, for another conversation was going on beneath the first. After a while Edd said, almost shyly, "I nearly forgot, I have a present for you," and from his pocket he pulled a tiny, heart-shaped box covered in red satin. Alice slowly untied the red ribbon from around the box, savoring each moment of anticipation, and removed the lid. "Oh, chocolate candy!" she smiled delightedly as she offered the box for him to take a piece. Their first awkwardness forgotten, they munched candy and talked and laughed contentedly as the afternoon flew past.

Edd stayed for supper, then left to return to Hartzlers after promising Alice a ride to church in the morning. For the next week, Edd saw Alice whenever he could arrange to do so. She had given up her winter job as a cook at the Commercial Hotel, for she was planning to leave for Oregon within a week. With no responsibilities other than to enjoy the time she had left in Missouri, Alice gave herself up to the pleasure of being courted attentively. Well-dressed and mannerly, Edd showed Alice an aspect of himself quite unlike the dusty "separator man" from the threshing crew. Alice glowed in a new light, too; her sweet face, pretty clothes, and vivacious personality made Edd proud to be with her.

On the Sunday before Alice left Garden City, Edd invited her to join the Hartzlers for dinner after church, then suggested an afternoon walk in the balmy spring sunshine. Lilacs perfumed the breeze as the couple strolled along the railroad tracks south of town; suddenly, a gust of wind flipped Alice's stylish hat from her head and tumbled it over and over along the ground. "Oh! Oh!" she cried in frustration, but she was soon laughing at Edd, who cut a comical figure chasing after it. He captured the wayward bonnet and handed it back to Alice with a flourish, making her laugh even more as she settled it firmly on her head and secured it with several large hat pins.

After they had walked for a while, chatting amiably about family and friends, Edd stopped beneath an old maple tree just beginning to unfurl tender new leaves and caught Alice's hands in his. Looking at her soberly, he asked, "Allie, my dear, would you consider marrying me and making a life with me in Dakota? I'd be awfully good to you, for I've come to love you a great deal."

"Oh, Edd," she said breathlessly, "I hardly know how to answer you. I can't marry you, you see, because you're not a Christian; my parents would never allow it. And then, I don't believe that they would want me to go so far from home with someone they've never met."

Her hands trembled in his as she went on. "I did love the Dakota prairies, but when I think of never seeing my dear sisters, my little brothers, and my father and mother again, I don't know whether I could bear it."

"But Allie, I will come back to the Mennonite church," Edd said. "I'd already planned to do that before you spoke. I've been thinking about it for some time and I'm ready to lead a different kind of life. You'll help me to do that, won't you?"

As Alice looked at him tenderly, he went on, "If you will marry me, I'll sell my land in Dakota and make a new life with you in Oregon; that's how much I want you, dear girl!"

COURTING

Alice's arms around his neck were her reply and Edd held her very close, feeling for the first time in his life that he was not alone.

A dapper Edd Yoder prepares to travel to Oregon to marry Alice Troyer.

CHAPTER 20: Oregon Bound

ALICE AGREED TO marry Edd the following December if her parents approved. She decided to return to Oregon immediately and break the news to her family when she felt the time was right. Meanwhile, Edd intended to work in North Dakota from spring planting through the fall threshing season, giving him time to sell his land and put his affairs in order. They would be apart for eight months unless Alice traveled to North Dakota to cook for the harvest crew, but it could not be helped. Even if Edd found buyers for his property, he could not hope for payment until the year's crops were sold.

Spring came late to Dakota that year, but Edd found no shortage of work when he arrived in Kenmare in May. Amos Ogburn offered him a job through harvest time; it included room and board and Edd was well pleased. He planted oats on his homestead claim and rejoiced when mild weather and frequent rains gave the crop a good start.

True to his word, Edd took steps to return to the Mennonite Church. Before leaving Missouri, he retrieved his membership letter from the church he had attended as a young boy during the family's brief sojourn in Garden City. He intended to carry the letter to Oregon and join a church there after he was married.

In Dakota, Edd began to regularly attend the Spring Valley Mennonite Church near Baden, and on the first Sunday in July, Independence Day, he was baptized by Brother Isaac Mast.

I made a confession of my sins to God, Edd wrote to Alice. *And oh, dear girl, do you know? I feel so much better. I didn't know what it was to be saved. I always thought that if I lived a moral life, that was enough. But I have found out different.*

Edd knew that the Mennonites held strong beliefs against the worldly ways that had been part of his life in Dakota. During his time in the North Woods he had acquired the lumberjacks' habit of chewing tobacco. In his coal mining days, he helped organize the first miners' unions and even held a seat on the union board. He'd also joined the Masons and had risen high in the ranks of that secret society. Now he found it surprisingly easy to give those things up.

One evening before the Masons' monthly meeting, Edd took the Lodge Master aside and asked for a private word. "I'm going to tender my resignation from the Lodge," Edd told the man. "I'm a Christian, I've recently been baptised into the Mennonite Church, and the church doesn't believe in belonging to societies such as the Masons. Surprised and displeased, at first the Lodge Master refused to accept Edd's resignation, arguing persuasively, then angrily, against his defection.

"You won't find the same doors open to you in this community, I warn you," the man harangued him. "You won't find it as easy to get ahead." Sure of his new direction and bolstered by his promises to Alice, however, Edd stood firm. "What you say may be true," he replied, "but I have found a better way to live."

OREGON BOUND

Edd also resolved to spend less time with friends whose habits he no longer wished to emulate. Thankfully, that resolve was eased by the fact that, one by one, the old gang was marrying and settling down.

Weddings, it seemed, were in the air. Otis Ogburn was courting the schoolteacher, Alice Best. Levi Yoder and Anna Harshbarger had set up housekeeping the previous fall. *And the first thing they did was go to Kauffman's [store] and buy some carrots, turnips, and other vegetables.* Edd wrote to Alice. *Hurrah for the soup! They are about the same as two little kittens: soup for breakfast, soup for dinner, and soup for supper!*

Cousin Joe Kauffman married Alice's dear friend, Agnes, and they were living with Aunt Mattie, whose health was failing. Then in rapid succession Ernest Squire, Coy Collins, and Sam Galyen all married and moved away from Kenmare — Ernest to Minnesota, Coy to Canada, and Sam many miles south to Belfield, North Dakota.

Alice did not immediately tell her parents about Edd's proposal, so he kept quiet about it, too, working hard and keeping his correspondence with Alice light and affectionate. Then, toward the middle of July, Edd stopped by the Baden store around noon and found a letter waiting for him. Although he recognized Alice's handwriting, he felt curiously reluctant to open the slender envelope. Instead, Edd tucked the letter inside his overalls and went back to work at Ogburn's, but all afternoon he felt its weight in his pocket.

After supper, Edd walked out to the barnyard and climbed onto the wagon seat. He turned the letter over in his hands several times. Giving himself a shake, as if to throw off his misgivings, he slit the envelope open with his pocketknife. For a long time after he read the brief missive, Edd sat hunched over on the wagon seat, his calloused hands dangling between his knees. Finally, in the gathering dusk, he pulled a small tablet of paper and a stubby pencil from his pocket and began a reply to Alice.

I hardly know what to say, he wrote. *I am so sorry that your mother opposes our marriage. Does she object very strong? What does your father say? And your sisters, what do they think? Tell your mother that the reasons we weren't together this summer was because I wanted to sell my land and collect what money I have out on interest so we could start out in fair circumstances. Tell her not to judge me by your brother-in-law that isn't doing well. Tell them to write to Amos (if nothing else will do) and ask him what kind of a person I am. Of course, if they won't give their consent, I don't know what to do unless I write to them or come out there myself. I do wish we could talk together. I am willing to do anything to convince your people that I will do my best and that I will work hard for you.*

A week later, Alice wrote that she had spoken only to her mother and that she hoped to convince her family over time. For a while, Edd felt reassured. But as the summer wore on, it became clear that her mother's opposition continued and that it was taking its toll on Alice. Hoping to enlist her sisters on her behalf, Alice brought them into the secret, but impressed on them that they must not tell their father, for she knew that if Amos refused her wishes now, that would end the engagement. Better to convince the rest of the family first, she decided, and present her father with a united front.

OREGON BOUND

The threshing season began, and hard work and worry leaned Edd down to a spare hundred and forty pounds. Alice wasn't there to ply him with extra cake, pie, and glasses of fresh milk, and the new cooks' culinary skills were indifferent. Then a letter from Ohio laid another burden on his heart: Edd's youngest sister, Anna, was stricken with typhoid. Exhausted and anxious, his natural optimism faltered beneath the strain.

So your mother still doesn't feel like giving her consent, he wrote to Alice. *I can't blame her at all, but I am so sorry. I think it can't be. Just about four months more until we intended to get married. I thought of what happiness was awaiting us both, and now it may all be shattered. I often think of when you were here last fall and how good and kind you always were to me. I surely never will forget your kindness.*

In the midst of his despair over the engagement, however, Edd sold the homestead portion of his land to Lee Kauffman for a top price of one thousand one hundred dollars, plus a share of the current year's crops. He also leased his remaining eighty acres to John Hooks, who immediately began to prepare it for winter wheat. As things began to go his way, Edd's successes bolstered his determination to travel to Oregon after the harvest and convince Alice's parents that he would make her a worthy husband.

Although no one in Ohio knew of the engagement, Edd's strained letters home soon brought his brother Dan to North Dakota. Edd was overjoyed to see his brother and relieved to hear that sister Anna was recovering from typhoid. Dan bunked with Edd in the shanty, along with Will Yoder and Dan Miller from the threshing crew, and the four men enjoyed a rowdy camaraderie

IN THE HOLLOW OF GOD'S HAND

A last, wintry look at Kenmare, North Dakota, on the shores of Des Lacs Lake, in December 1909.

that raised Edd's spirits and distracted him from his concerns about his future with Alice.

The men finished threshing on the twenty-fifth of October. When Edd stopped at the Baden store on his way home that night, a letter was waiting. He had not written to Alice for a month, and apprehension tensed his muscles as he tore open the envelope. As he read, his exhausted body sagged against the back wall of the store. When he finished the letter and raised his eyes, tears were streaming from them.

My parents have given their consent to our marriage, Alice wrote, *and in my next letter I will be able to tell you a date.*

At last, they could begin to plan their life together. Now the letters flew thick and fast between Oregon and North Dakota. Edd

OREGON BOUND

left it to Alice to set the wedding date and make the arrangements — *only let me know a few weeks before the time*, he wrote — but he sent money to pay for a traditional wedding supper. Alice was working in Portland and beseeched Edd to come to Oregon as soon as possible to spend some time with her before the wedding. Now that the outcome was assured, however, Edd lingered in Dakota, concluding his land business, ordering a handsome black wedding suit, and enjoying his brother's company. But when the land contracts had been drawn up, the suit was finished, and Dan had left for Ohio, Edd knew that it was time to go.

The wedding was set for the twelfth of December. Fearing that winter storms might delay him, Edd set out for Oregon on December 2. As the train steamed out of Kenmare, sadness at leaving the prairies he loved struggled with thoughts of future happiness with Alice. So much was unknown. Would her family accept him? Could they make a success of farming? How would he like Oregon? Would their life together be blessed or barren? All of his worldly goods were packed in a truck stowed in the baggage car and in a carry-on valise. An envelope containing a bank draft rested in his pocket. Suddenly it seemed very little with which to start a marriage.

Edd broke his journey in Spokane, Washington. Reluctant to arrive in the midst of the wedding preparations, he decided to rest a couple of days and look up a cousin, Ben Yoder. But alone in a hotel room, his apprehensions overcame him, and he sat all day looking out the window at Spokane's dusty streets and thinking about Alice. All his hopes and dreams now rested on this slender, twenty-one-year-old woman, in whose company he had actually spent only a few weeks. When he could no longer bear his lonely thoughts, he wrote a last letter to Alice from the road.

This has been a blue day for me, but then there are bright days coming, aren't there? I wish you were here to spend the evening with me. My room has a bed, washstand, chair, rocking chair, pictures on the wall, wardrobe, lace curtains, and electric lights. But the best of all is not here, and that is Alice. If you were here, everything would be first class. I will leave for Portland Wednesday evening and get there Thursday morning at 9 o'clock, if I keep well, and to Hubbard Friday evening. I can't hardly wait until I meet you again.

Carefully he folded the letter and placed it in an envelope, ready to mail the next morning. He undressed methodically and hung his clothes in the wardrobe. The room felt overheated, so he opened the window a few inches, turned out the electric light, and got into bed. The darkness pressed down on him and in desperation he prayed, over and over: *Let me be all that I can be to her; let me make the best of this new life.*

At last, he slept.

PART TWO

The Peace Church

*"Peace I leave with you,
my peace I give unto you:
not as the world giveth, give I unto you.
Let not your heart be troubled,
neither let it be afraid."*
— JOHN 14:27

*"[We] do not go to war nor fight.
[We] are the children of peace who have beaten our
swords into plowshares and our spears
into pruning hooks and know of no war."*
— MENNO SIMONS

Alice Pearl, sixth child of Amos and Delilah (Lyle) Troyer.

CHAPTER 21: The Bishop's Daughter

ALICE'S LIFE HAD BEEN ONE of peace and plenty. Her parents, Amos and Delilah Troyer, were prosperous Amish–Mennonite farmers who, in 1892, sold their land near Garden City, Missouri, loaded their livestock, household goods, and farm implements onto an immigrant train, and moved their family of eight children to Oregon. Alice was three years old when the family arrived in Oregon's verdant Willamette Valley.

Amos had been suffering from the after-effects of typhoid for some time, and Delilah believed that Missouri's climate was not healthful for him. When friends returned from a trip to the Pacific Northwest and extolled the region's rich soils and abundant crops, Delilah vowed to see the West for herself. She bought a ticket to the Willamette Valley and embarked on a reconnaissance mission. In Oregon, she found what she believed to be a farmer's paradise, and when she returned to Garden City she soon convinced Amos to emigrate.

Delilah, nicknamed Lyle, was a skilled herbalist. From Missouri, she brought her medicine chest, medical books, and a pair of forceps for extracting teeth. She used garden herbs and homeopathic remedies purchased from a Portland, Oregon, drugstore to doctor her family and friends. Dr. Schoor, a local physician who had emigrated from Missouri shortly after the Troyers, frequently consulted with her on difficult cases.

In the Willamette Valley, the Troyers settled into a two-storey, seventeen-room house on six hundred and forty acres of rolling farmland. Near the house, a large Amish-style bank barn, built against a slope for easy entry on two levels, sheltered livestock, hay, and grain. The family quickly assimilated into the Amish–Mennonite community and within a year, Amos was ordained bishop of the Rock Creek Church. He later held the positions of deacon (chosen by lot), and then bishop (also chosen by lot), in the new Zion Mennonite Church, which was built in 1898.

An Amish–Mennonite bishop not only led his congregation, he was its chief authority in spiritual matters. He preached the main sermon, administered communion and baptism, performed marriages and announced excommunications (the dreaded shunning), and reinstated backsliding church members. He also supervised the choosing of ministers by lot and performed ordinations. Although Amos's position in the church elevated his family's stature in the rapidly growing community, it also imposed restrictions: his wife and children must always be above reproach in word and deed, lest they reflect poorly on his leadership.

After the move to Oregon, Lyle birthed two more daughters and two sons; however, one of the baby girls lived only a year. Still, the seven girls — Elizabeth, Sarah, Nora, Grace, Ida, Alice, and Emma and three boys — Jesse, Ernest, and Daniel — filled the big farmhouse to overflowing. Alice Pearl, the sixth child, was her father's favorite. From the beginning, her intelligence, vivacity, and love of music stood out in the busy household.

THE BISHOP'S DAUGHTER

But every eye in the community looked to the Troyers to set an example of sober, Godly living, and Alice sometimes chaffed at the restrictions imposed by her father's position.

Inevitably, Alice's yearning for music got her into trouble.

Amish–Mennonites forbade playing musical instruments other than mouth organs, and all singing must be *a capella*: voice only. But Alice longed to make music using more than her lovely voice. She saved pennies and dimes earned from doing housework for friends and relatives and bought an inexpensive guitar from one of her schoolmates. She smuggled the guitar into the barn's hayloft and practiced playing it only when her father was away from home or working in the fields far from the house.

One afternoon, Father Amos rode in from the fields to mend a broken harness strap. As he dismounted his horse, he heard guitar music cascading from behind the barn. He hurried around the corner to see who was breaking the ironclad code of conduct and saw to his dismay that it was his favorite child, little Alice. Because Alice had not yet joined the church, some leniency would normally be called for. But leniency was out of the question in the case of the bishop's daughter. No whisper of wrongdoing must ever be attached to the Troyer family. So, regretfully, Amos lifted the offending guitar from his daughter's hands and broke it into splinters over his knee. As he turned away from Alice's defiantly dry-eyed gaze, however, his own eyes filled with tears.

On a summer Sunday in 1900, after Amos preached the sermon at Zion Church, twelve young people walked to a spring-fed stream behind the church to be baptized. Twelve-year-old Alice and her best friend, Mary Miller, gripped each other's hands and gazed at the sun-dappled water as they waited their turn. At last, Alice waded into the shallow pool and her father performed the solemn ritual. Now her life was dedicated to serving God and she vowed never to waver from that path.

Alice's music, still a cornerstone of her life, could be explored only within the context of religious service, so she began to sing in the annual Christmas choir, then later sang duets with her sister Lizzie at Sunday services. Alice's voice had a stunning range: she could sing any part from alto to tenor to soprano.

In winter, in addition to her regular schooling, Alice joined other Amish–Mennonite children at an informal German School held by Samuel Roth. There she learned to read and write the language that was primary in the church and still spoken in many households. In the Troyer home, the children spoke German to their father and English to their mother.

For all her external conformity to the Amish–Mennonite way of living, Alice's independent and adventurous nature continually sought to fly free of its constraints. In the fall of 1903, sister Lizzie married Daniel Hostetler, and just over a year later sister Grace married John Berkey. As nieces and nephews began to arrive, Alice often stayed at one of her sisters' homes to help with babies and housework. At eighteen, when she had the opportunity to work in a bakery in the rapidly growing metropolis of Portland and room with her Aunt Sarah Yoder, Alice took the job without a moment's hesitation.

At first, Alice found the bustling city daunting after her quiet country home, but she quickly became accustomed to the streetcar's rumble interwoven with the shrill blare of automobile horns, the ring of horseshoes on brick and macadam, and the deafening rattle of countless buggies and wagons. The lively streets flowed with a rich and varied tide of humanity that washed up on the bakery's benign shore to be waited on by a sparkling-eyed Alice. Up before dawn to help bake the shop's breads, pies, cakes, and rolls, Alice's seemingly boundless energy kept her going through the morning rush and into the afternoon flow of exhausted shoppers, who eased their aching limbs on a handful of ornately scrolled iron chairs as they munched cookies and cinnamon rolls and sipped coffee or tea.

Her vivacity also began to attract young men, who vied for the privilege of walking Alice home from church or taking her buggy riding. One man in particular, Frank Zook, was utterly smitten, and Alice returned his regard. As they spent more and more time together, they lightheartedly began to talk about a shared future. Often they joked and laughed as they built dream castles in the air. Alice liked nice things, and working in Portland had exposed her to worldly delights never thought of in her plain home. One day when Frank and Alice were discussing the kind of house they'd like to live in, Alice described her choice of parlor furnishings in great detail.

"We're going to have red velvet curtains!" she exclaimed.

"Yes, and we'll have some little Chinamen that will wait on us, too!" cried Frank, not to be outdone.

In the winter of 1907–08, several Mennonite young people from North Dakota traveled west to visit relatives in Oregon. One of them, Agnes Andrews, became fast friends with Alice.

When it was time for Agnes to return home she pleaded with Alice to accompany her.

"We'll have such fun, you can't imagine," Agnes urged. "And you really ought to see a little of the world before you settle down with Frank!" It didn't take much discussion to convince Alice, who had money saved from her work in the bakery, that the trip would be an adventure she would relish. And besides, Frank hadn't actually proposed. Maybe some time apart would bring him to the point, Alice thought tartly.

Convincing Alice's parents to let her go so far away wasn't easy, but the Troyers had relations and friends all along the journey's route and everyone thought well of Agnes. So the trip began to take shape. The girls would spend time in Idaho with cousins before continuing on to North Dakota. On the return trip, Alice planned to travel through Missouri and perhaps meet Amos and Delilah there for the journey back to Oregon.

In May, when the weather warmed and the threat of snow at higher elevations waned, the congenial group of young people gathered their belongings and, in a flurry of farewells, boarded an eastbound train. If anyone had told Alice, as she seated herself in the plush Pullman car with unconcealed delight, that she would not see her home again for an entire year, and that when she returned to Oregon she would be secretly engaged to marry a man she had yet to meet, she would have laughed in disbelief. But the journey was to be a fateful one.

THE BISHOP'S DAUGHTER

Alice Troyer, left, with dear friend Agnes Andrews, who convinced Alice to travel to North Dakota. Agnes later married Edd's cousin Joe Kauffman.

CHAPTER 22: Alice's Secret

TRAVELING BEYOND THE GRAND, snow-covered Cascade Mountain range, across Idaho's wind-scoured Great Basin lands, through the magnificent Rockies, and over the endless steppes of Eastern Montana and North Dakota left Alice feeling that she had journeyed a very long way, and not only geographically. Harsh pioneer conditions still predominated across those lands, and although Agnes's friends and family welcomed her warmly, Alice found North Dakota life more primitive than what she was used to. Alice enjoyed herself with Agnes, but it wasn't long before time began to hang heavily on her hands and she began to look around for something to occupy her time.

Now a widow, Mattie Kauffman needed help with her housework and vegetable garden, so Agnes and Alice often spent a day at the Kauffman farm. Alice's cooking and baking skills were soon much in demand, and a gathering of the Kauffman clan for Sunday dinner at Mattie's with Alice presiding in the kitchen was all it took to convince Mattie's son, Lee, that she would make a fine cook for the harvest crew. When he offered her the job, Alice agreed without a moment's hesitation. Capably, she immediately began planning meals and considering what supplies she would need to feed a perpetually hungry crew for several weeks.

Out of sympathy for the Harshbarger family's straitened circumstances, Lee also hired Anna Harshbarger to help with the cooking. When Alice met Anna she was taken aback at the young woman's boisterous personality, but under Alice's soft-spoken directives the two women quickly settled into a congenial routine. Hard work and long hours made the weeks fly past, and well before she was ready for it to end, Alice's time in North Dakota drew to a close.

Alice had enjoyed her breezy friendship with crew foreman Edd Yoder, and she found herself hoping he might drop by the cook car on her last morning at the farm. He didn't appear, however, so she tucked her disappointment away and focused on her journey to Missouri.

At Kenmare, she boarded the Great Northern cars to Minneapolis, then changed to another railway line that took her south though Iowa to Kansas City, Missouri, where she transferred to the Kansas City, Clinton & Springfield Railroad. The KCC&S was called the "Leaky Roof Line" because it often commandeered the oldest and leakiest railcars to haul clay tile, which was impervious to water. One rainy day those battered cars had showed up at the Clinton flour mill, causing the plant foreman to exclaim, "We won't ship out any flour today, they've sent us another batch of 'leaky roofs!'" To the railway owners' consternation, the nickname stuck.

With some trepidation, Alice boarded a passenger car, noting with relief that it seemed dry and well appointed. She settled herself quickly on the comfortable seat, eager to traverse the final few miles of her journey. When at last her train pulled into

ALICE'S SECRET

Garden City, the weary traveler was overjoyed to find her parents waiting for her on the tiny station platform. First her father, then her mother caught her up in warm hugs that left Alice's eyes brimming. It seemed like many more than five months since she had seen her dear parents. Her eyes still blurred with happy tears, Alice joined Amos and Delilah in an open spring wagon for the winding six-mile drive to the small settlement of La Tour and the home of Troyer relatives. Although the fall air held a chill, it felt much warmer than Dakota, and Alice noticed that brilliantly colored autumn leaves still clothed many of the trees.

The family had much news to share, so the next few days were lively ones. When Amos and Delilah left for Oregon, however, Alice stayed behind. She had decided to spend a few months in Missouri with the Troyer clan, for she was enjoying her adventurous new life and imagined that her return to Oregon might be the end of her journeying. Then, too, Edd's married sister Lydia lived in Garden City, so the chances of seeing him again were greatly improved. Although she scarcely admitted the latter inducement to herself, the thought rested comfortably in a corner of her mind.

As soon as her parents headed west, Alice wrote to Edd and was pleasantly surprised when he responded immediately with an outpouring of news and a genial sharing of his plans for the winter. She lost no time in penning a warm response and a weekly flow of letters began. Edd's lighthearted but well-written missives reminisced about their good times in North Dakota and, once he returned to Ohio, kept her abreast of the news there, but little in them suggested anything other than friendship. The letters never failed to arrive weekly, however, and they always ended with a plea for her to write soon.

Drawn to Oregon's milder climate and richer soils, several Troyer families sold their Missouri farms and headed West early in the New Year. Determined to see the winter through in Missouri, however, Alice went to stay with relatives in Garden City. Sewing for her cousin Dora Troyer, cooking and doing housework for the Amos Martin family, and working in the Commercial Hotel's kitchen ensured her financial independence and garnered funds for her trip home.

Alice seldom heard from Frank Zook, her Oregon beau, and when he did write she found his letters not nearly as much to her liking as Edd's. She thought of Edd so often, in fact, that in February she wrote and encouraged him to travel to Oregon with her and her cousins. Edd's response was both gratifying and frustrating. He thanked Alice warmly for the invitation, but hesitated to say yes because *I hardly know anyone out there and maybe I couldn't get work.* Still, he questioned her about the group she would be traveling with and expressed hopes of seeing her when he arrived in Missouri in April. He also urged her to send a long-promised photograph. And for the first time, rather than "Your Friend," he signed his letter simply "Yours."

Alice's heart quickened as her eyes scanned the pages. Suddenly she wanted very much to see Edd again and she vowed to stay in Missouri until he arrived, despite imploring letters from home to return for sister Ida's rapidly approaching wedding. Somehow, over the winter, Edd had become firmly ensconced in Alice's heart, and now she longed to see him in person to determine whether he was all she remembered him to be. She continued to encourage Edd to visit Missouri and promised him her company when he did arrive.

At last, after a flurry of sweeter and sweeter missives, came the letter she had been waiting for; Edd was on his way. Then he was at her door, and soon they were in the parlor chatting like dear friends — yet so much more, Alice thought joyfully, trying hard to breathe evenly and not reveal how overwhelmed she felt at seeing him again. Strikingly handsome in his well-cut suit, Edd scarcely resembled the dust-covered "separator man" of the harvest fields. At twenty-seven he was mature, experienced, well traveled, and self-educated; far different from the boys Alice knew back home. That he cared for her was obvious, and each meeting deepened the connection they both felt. But now Alice found herself in a quandary; what was to come of this powerful attraction?

Within days, her question was answered. When Edd proposed marriage, practical Alice, the bishop's daughter and revered father's favorite child, reluctantly gave him the only answer she could. Her heart beating as rapidly as birds' wings, caged by the dutiful reality of her life, Alice told him "No."

Earnestly, Edd pleaded with her to reconsider, promising to do whatever he could to ensure her happiness and prove his worth to her parents. When at last he caught her up in his arms, Alice's "No" had become "Yes," and when their lips met in a sweet and passionate kiss, Alice gave her heart as fully as Edd had already pledged his.

IN THE HOLLOW OF GOD'S HAND

Alice's friends and traveling companions included cousins Dora and Cora Troyer, front left *and* middle. *Alice is third from left in back row.*

The trip home to Oregon sandwiched between chattering cousins Dora and Cora passed in a blur. The three women nearly missed the train from Garden City on the Monday morning of their departure, but Alice scarcely noticed, so caught up was she in thinking about the previous day's events. How would she manage to keep such a huge secret, she wondered? It wouldn't do to tell anyone until she spoke with her parents in case they were against the marriage. Alice mailed Edd a hastily scribbled postcard when she changed trains in Denver, but not knowing who might see it en route she kept her message light and ambiguous.

So begins my secret life, she thought, with a shiver of dismay; how will it all end?

CHAPTER 23: Opposition and Inner Turmoil

BACK AT HOME, ALICE SCARCELY knew how to broach the subject of Edd and marriage to her parents, so for a time she simply kept the news to herself. Edd continued to write every week, and if his letters were not as full of plans for the future as she wished, they at least told her that he was working, he thought of her, and he missed her. When Frank Zook came calling, she faced the difficult task of dashing his hopes that she was still his girl.

"I can't tell you much about it yet because I haven't discussed it with my parents," Alice told Frank honestly, "but I hope to marry someone else before the year is over, and so I must not go out with you again."

"But we can still be good friends, can't we?" Frank pleaded. "I can still take you to church and young people's meeting and such, can't I? At least let me keep seeing you until you're sure you'll be married."

"No, Frank, that can't be," Alice said sadly. "We've cared for each other too much and it wouldn't be right to go on as we used to when I'm promised to someone else."

So, reluctantly, Frank stayed away, but now and then he wrote Alice a note to remind her that he still thought of her.

Concerned about money for her wedding dress, the wedding supper, and the clothes she would need after she was married, Alice immediately went to work, and the long summer days of labor from daylight to dark blurred together, punctuated only by Sunday services and Edd's weekly letters. At last Edd wrote of his conversion and baptism; the same letter told of his plans to sell his land in Dakota. He was true to his word; now, Alice must do her part.

As Alice sat with her mother on the porch shelling peas for the noon meal, she decided it was time to speak. Her twenty-first birthday was only a few days away, and soon she would no longer be subject to her parents' directives. But as a dutiful daughter and a member of the church, she could not go against their wishes.

"Mother, I've something to tell you, and I hope it will be good news," Alice began carefully. "When I was in North Dakota, I met a truly wonderful man, Edd Yoder, and we became friends. You know, he's Lydia Hartzler's brother. We wrote to each other all last winter, and this spring, when Edd came to visit his sister in Garden City, we spent more time together and, well, he asked me to marry him."

Delilah sat quietly, listening, as Alice rushed on.

"He owns land in North Dakota, but he is willing to sell it and move here to be with me. He wanted to come to Oregon with me this summer, but thought it best to work where he had a job and try to sell his property. We thought —" she paused and looked beseechingly at her mother, "well, if you and Pa approve, we thought we'd like to be married by the end of the year."

Relieved to have the situation out in the open at last, Alice leaned back in her chair with a sigh and waited for her mother to speak.

"I don't quite know what to say," Delilah spoke slowly. "I thought you and Frank — well, never mind about that, but you can hardly know this Edd Yoder, and your Pa and I don't know him at all. I don't see how we can give permission under those circumstances. But let me consider for a while. I think it's best that we don't tell your Pa just yet," she concluded.

Noticing Alice's distraught expression, Delilah decided to question her further.

"You haven't said whether he's a Christian, or how old he is, or what his circumstances are," Delilah queried.

"He is a Christian, a Mennonite who has come back to the church after a time away," Alice said eagerly. "He's a farmer, he has a homestead claim and some acreage besides, and he ran the threshing crew for Levi Kauffman last fall. He seems quite successful and highly regarded. As for his age —" she paused, "he's a little older than me, I think, um, I'm not exactly sure," she said, crestfallen at not knowing something so simple about the man she wanted to spend her life with.

Delilah drew back and looked at Alice searchingly, "You see, dear girl, you don't know him very well. There may be many more important things than his age that you don't know. I think we will let the subject rest there, and I advise you to look more closely at the fine young men in our church before you toss them all aside for this North Dakota stranger."

The two women sat in silence until the peas were finished; then Alice rose, carried the enameled dishpan into the kitchen, set it on the scrubbed wooden table, and went to the room she shared with her sisters. The room was empty, so she retrieved her pencil and a pad of paper from the dresser and wrote a brief letter to Edd. Still reeling emotionally from the conversation with her mother, Alice decided not to reveal Delilah's objections to their plans. Instead, she told Edd how happy she was that he had made a new start in life by returning to the church. She also asked his age, though embarrassed to do so, and told him that she would be twenty-one years old on July 9. At last, then, her emotions took over, and she wrote how much she missed him and how she wished they could have had this summer together to get to know each other better. It was not quite an admonishment, but a little part of her wondered whether Edd *could* have managed to come to Oregon if he'd wanted to spend the summer with her badly enough. Wearily she sealed the envelope, addressed and stamped it, and put it in her pocket ready to drop in the mailbox later that day.

Delilah made a Martha Washington layer cake for Alice's birthday, and her brothers and sisters gathered around the supper table to wish her well. But little sister Emma, her dearest confidant, noticed that Alice seemed subdued. Later that evening Em found Alice alone on the porch and slipped her hand into her sister's.

"You haven't seemed like your usual happy self this summer," Em said, looking at Alice's face, a pale oval in the twilight. "Did something happen in Missouri to put you in glum spirits?"

"Oh, Em!" Alice couldn't hold the news inside any longer. "Edd Yoder asked me to marry him, and after awhile I told him

OPPOSITION AND INNER TURMOIL

'yes' if Mom and Papa didn't object and if he would come to Oregon to live. But when I told mother about him a few days ago she said she didn't see how they could agree to my marrying someone they didn't even know. What am I going to do?"

Emma squeezed her sister's hand tightly in sympathy. "Do you love him?" she asked solemnly.

"Yes, I do," Alice replied, "And it's hard that he's so far away. I know he's doing what he thinks is right for us, working this summer in Dakota and trying to get his affairs in order, but I don't think he understands how much difference it would make if he were here."

"I think you should let him know that mother objects to the marriage," Emma advised practically, "and maybe he will come to Oregon sooner and then it will all work out."

CHAPTER 24: Love Finds a Way

ALICE FOLLOWED EMMA'S SUGGESTION and wrote to Edd about her mother's reaction to the proposed marriage. Stunned and disappointed, Edd nevertheless responded lovingly and reassuringly. He believed that they would eventually win her parents over, and he vowed to come to Oregon to do so if necessary. Gratefully, Alice sent him her photograph and a small basket of ripe Oregon cherries and tried to reassure him in return. *I won't give up,* she wrote, *I will keep trying to convince them.*

Alice worked away from home until mid-August and then took a few weeks off to help her mother with the late-summer fruit and vegetable canning. As the two women labored side by side, Alice again broached the subject of marrying Edd, and again her mother refused to consider it.

"Nothing has changed since we last talked about this, Alice," Delilah said emphatically, "and I don't want to hear any more about it."

By now, Alice had confided in her sisters, but she still hesitated to tell her father. Except for sister Ida, who had always been jealous of Alice, the young women all supported Alice's plans. Still, she worried and prayed about the situation until she could scarcely think of anything else. She lost weight and grew pale and quiet. After Delilah's second refusal, Edd's emotional distress also increased, and his letters vacillated between encouraging Alice to follow her heart and counseling her to respect her parents' wishes.

September began, bringing a break from the summer's heat and hard work, and the Troyers planned a camping trip to the Oregon Coast. The journey took three days by wagon, traveling along winding dirt roads through the Coast Range and stopping occasionally to pick wild huckleberries while keeping an eye out for the black bears that would be feasting in the berry thickets.

On their second night out, a snarling scream jolted Alice awake. She sat bolt upright in the women's tent as the scream rent the darkness once again and Emma clutched Delilah in fright. Alice crawled to the tent flap and peaked out just as her father emerged from the men's tent clutching his rifle. Amos ran to where the horses were rearing, snorting, and trying desperately to jerk their picket ropes from the ground. Another scream, much closer, and Amos jacked a shell into the rifle's chamber and fired; as he did so a long, tawny shape, pale gold in the starlight, stretched downward from a big-leaf maple's thick branches and slid into the shadows at the clearing's edge.

"What was that, Pa?" Alice called softly, and Pa replied, "A mountain lion, Alice. It was after the horses. But don't worry, it's gone now, and I'll keep watch for a while."

Halcyon coastal days and invigorating walks along the ocean refreshed Alice and calmed her agitated thoughts, but when she returned home the internal pressure to resolve the situation with her beau filled her head like a balloon about to burst. Edd was laboring in the harvest fields now, and for the first time since Alice left Dakota a year ago, his weekly letters did not come. In desperation, Alice approached her father one evening as he stood in the twilight, leaning against the fence rail and looking out across newly shorn fields.

"Oh Papa," she began, when a flood of tears suddenly overwhelmed her. Her father's big arms went around her and cradled her as she cried helplessly.

"What is it, Alice?" Amos asked at last. "What has been troubling you for so long?"

As the story rolled out through her tears, Amos listened closely, and when she was finished he questioned her gravely, "Are you very sure, Alice, that this Edd Yoder will make you happy?"

"Yes, Pa, I am," she replied. "He is a kind man and a hard worker, and I have no doubt that we will have a good life together."

"Then I am satisfied." Amos said. "I trust my girl's good judgment. Let us talk with your mother and we will work it out."

Nevertheless, October was nearly over before Alice was able to give Edd the joyful news: Amos and Delilah had given their blessing and the wedding plans could go forward. Alice set the date for December 12, her father's birthday, and the couple began a flurry of preparations. Alice decided to work in Portland for the month of November and she begged Edd to travel west immediately to spend time with her before the wedding. Now that the event was assured, however, Edd delayed in Kenmare to wrap up his land deals and purchase a wedding suit. In truth, given their initial opposition, Edd imagined that the less time he spent with Alice's family before the wedding, the better.

Still not totally convinced that the event would take place, Edd told no one in North Dakota or Ohio of his plans. Soon enough to tell them when it's done, he thought, as he quietly readied himself for departure. Edd waited to close his bank account until one of the younger tellers who didn't know him manned the window. As he tucked a bank draft for three hundred dollars into the inside pocket of his oldest jacket, he congratulated himself that no one would be the wiser if things went awry.

LOVE FINDS A WAY

Edward Z. Yoder and Alice Pearl Troyer were married December 12, 1909.

CHAPTER 25: The Wedding

SHE PLANNED TO BE MARRIED AT HOME, so Alice spent some of her hard-earned money on rolls of crepe paper to decorate the front sitting room. On the Friday before the wedding, sister Emma helped her stretch colorful crepe paper streamers from a large paper bell hung in the center of the parlor outward to the room's four corners. When at last they finished, Alice clapped her hands delightedly at the result just as her father passed the door on his way to dinner.

"What's this?" Amos asked in astonishment. "Why have you decorated the parlor?"

"It's for the wedding ceremony, Pa," Alice replied happily. "We'll stand below the bell in the center of the room and the guests can all gather 'round us."

"Alice, this cannot be," Amos said emphatically. "How will it look to have the bishop's daughter married at home, surrounded by such worldly trappings, rather than in the church, humbly and plainly before God? No, you must take all these decorations down immediately. You will be married at Zion and I will hear no argument about it."

After a nearly silent dinner, Alice returned to the parlor and pulled down all of the paper streamers. She took down the paper bell, folded its accordion pleats, and laid it away in a drawer. Emma came into the parlor as she finished and gave Alice a sympathetic hug.

"Look, Alice, you've left a little piece of crepe paper stuck up in the corner," Emma pointed out.

"I know it, Em," Alice replied, "and I'm going to leave it there, too, just for spite. In fact, I think I'll call that my spite corner," she said, ruefully. "But anyway, I don't have time to think about it now; Edd is arriving in Hubbard on the evening train and I must get ready to meet him."

A few hours later, Alice huddled next to her father on the wagon seat as the horses trotted briskly west along Whiskey Hill Road. Late-afternoon shadows darkened the muddy ruts and cold, damp December air swirled heavily around them. Well wrapped against the chill, Alice still shivered a little from nervousness and excitement. When at last the wagon rolled down Second Street to the Hubbard Depot, winter twilight had gathered the bustling town in its folds and the gas streetlamps wore misty haloes. A distant rumble heralded the rapidly approaching Southern Pacific engine and passenger cars. Alice's arms hugged her upper body beneath her heavy woolen cloak as she tried to stand quietly beside her father's burly frame. She peeked sideways at his inscrutable features and tension coiled tighter in her stomach as the steaming train ground to a halt.

The conductor emerged first from the passenger car, then — oh! there he was, just as she remembered, a delighted grin splitting his handsome face. Alice stepped forward eagerly to

THE WEDDING

meet Edd as he dropped his valise and caught both her hands in his. Together they turned toward Amos as Alice breathlessly introduced the two men. A quick glance to gauge her father's reaction loosened the knot in Alice's stomach: Amos seemed well disposed to Edd's sincere greeting. Then she had eyes only for her fiancé as they went about the business of retrieving Edd's steamer trunk and loading it into the wagon.

The long miles home in the cold darkness seemed short to Alice, wedged warmly between Edd and her father on the wagon seat with Edd's arm cozily wrapped around her shoulders. She listened to the men talk about farming, crops, and land prices, content to savor the closeness of her husband-to-be and feel the misty night air cooling her flushed face. At the Troyer farm, Delilah and the rest of the family welcomed the newcomer before they all sat down to a late supper. Edd would be bunking with Alice's brothers for two nights until the wedding. After the ceremony, the couple planned to go to the Woodburn Hotel for a brief honeymoon. Alice had hoped for a trip to the Coast or Portland, but she knew that Edd preferred to use their money to set up a home together, so the nearby hotel seemed a reasonable compromise.

Sunday, December 12, dawned clear and bitingly cold. Alice dressed carefully in her white wedding dress and beribboned slippers, and her best friend, Lomie Detweiler, helped her put the finishing touches on her hair and clothing. Delilah, Amos, and the rest of the family had gone ahead to the church, but in keeping with tradition Alice, Edd, and their two attendants planned to arrive right before the sermon began.

When they were ready to go, Alice joined Edd in the parlor for a moment, catching her breath in delight when she saw how dapper he looked in his black wedding suit.

"Are you happy, Allie?" Edd asked, as he held her hands in his.

"Oh yes, and a little nervous, too," she admitted. "It feels like a wonderful dream."

Lomie hurried into the parlor, then, to remind them that it was time to go.

The two couples walked sedately to the plain wooden church building, which sat at the edge of the Troyer farm, and stood outside on the porch until the congregation begin to sing a hymn. Edd held the door open for Lomie and her beau, Chauncey Kropf, and he and Alice followed them down the aisle to the reserved front bench. After the sermon, the congregation sang #295 in the black church hymnal, "Jesus A Wedding Guest," as Edd and Alice rose and stood before Amos, with Lomie and Chauncey on either side. The simple words of the wedding service were soon spoken, and Amos pronounced the couple husband and wife.

The wedding party happily led the way out of the church and down the path to the big Troyer farmhouse, where a traditional wedding dinner reposed on tables set throughout the downstairs rooms. Edd had paid for the hearty repast and for the specially selected servers who waited on the guests; now, he and Alice took their places at the head table and gratefully relaxed as family and friends joined them in celebration.

In the middle of each table, footed glass celery holders

THE WEDDING

sprouted a few precious stalks of the leafy green vegetable, unearthed from the winter storage cellar and displayed as a symbol of new beginnings. Surrounding the celery bouquets were platters of roast chicken and dressing; bowls of creamed vegetables and mashed potatoes; dishes of fruit salad, pickles, and a preserved vegetable relish called chow-chow; platters of breads and cookies; and of course, pies: fruit pies, shoo-fly pie, and Edd's favorite half-moon pies. After the first round of eating, the guests continued visiting, occasionally interrupting their reminiscences to sing a few traditional hymns; then came more eating, visiting, and singing.

Late in the afternoon the wedding couple slipped away to the barn, where their valises were tucked into the buggy that Alice's brother, Jesse, had hitched up and made ready for their departure. They settled themselves on the narrow buggy seat and Edd tucked a lap robe cozily around their heavy winter clothing. When he was certain that Alice was snugly wrapped, Edd slapped the reins across the horse's back and sent the buggy rolling down the road toward their new life together.

CHAPTER 26: Stealing a March

EDD AND ALICE SAT ACROSS from each other in the hotel dining room, enjoying a bountiful breakfast of hot biscuits and home cured ham and blissfully, if a little shyly, planning their first day together.

"I'd like to open a bank account this morning and deposit the draft I brought with me from Dakota," Edd said. "Then we ought to visit the lumberyard and look at house plans so that we can start building soon on that fifteen acres your father gave us for a wedding present. Do you think your brothers and sisters will mind that he's deeding those acres over to us?" he worried.

"No one needs to know that the property was a gift," Alice reassured him. "As far as they're concerned, you bought the land from Pa and that's the end of it. How soon do you think we can move into our own place?" she asked. "It's generous of my parents to let us stay with them until our house is built, but I won't feel altogether married until we're on our own."

"We'll start building as soon as the weather permits," Edd promised. "Of course, I'll need to till and plant a few acres come spring, so that may slow me down on the building, but we'll move as soon as I can manage it. In the meantime, we'll at least buy our own bedroom furniture so that we're not beholden to your folks for everything."

After breakfast, Edd and Alice window-shopped along Front Street as they strolled toward the bank. Woodburn appeared to be a prosperous town, Edd observed. Alice told him that after a catastrophic fire the town fathers had mandated all-brick construction, and the well-appointed two-storey brick buildings along Front Street now offered a wealth of goods and services. The Woodburn Hotel, set a block off Front Street on Garfield Street, boasted two floors of comfortable accommodations, with a north-facing inset upper gallery for sitting and strolling. The hotel served excellent meals, too.

When they reached the Farmers and Mechanics' Bank, Edd guided Alice to the manager's desk. They seated themselves on two wooden chairs and waited until the manager looked up from his paperwork and greeted them.

"I'd like to open an account and deposit a draft from the First National Bank of Kenmare, North Dakota," Edd began, unbuttoning his overcoat and pulling a long leather wallet from the inner pocket.

"Certainly, sir," the manager said, and he began taking papers from a desk drawer as Edd opened his wallet. The manager stopped abruptly, however, when Edd gave an exclamation of dismay.

"What is it, Edd," Alice asked in concern.

"The bank draft — it's not in my wallet," Edd exclaimed. "I'm certain I put it there when the teller gave it to me in Kenmare."

Edd sat still for a moment, a perplexed expression on his face, then he excused himself to the manager. "Sorry to have taken your time," he apologized. "We'll be back when I've located that draft." He rose, buttoned his overcoat, and took Alice's arm. "Good day to you."

"No problem, sir," the bank manager said as he ushered them to the door. "If there's anything I can do to help you, let me know, won't you?"

Outside the bank, Alice clutched his arm. "Oh Edd, what are you going to do?" she asked.

"Alice, do you know where the telegraph office is located?" Edd asked, trying to hide his agitation. "I'm going to send a telegram to the bank in Kenmare asking them to stop payment on that draft." And let's hope that it's not too late, he added to himself.

The day's plans were forgotten. After Edd sent his telegram from the train depot, he and Alice walked back to the hotel room and spent the day reading and trying to talk of anything but the missing draft. Despite their efforts, the loss of so much money cast a heavy gloom over both of them.

At last, after a long silence, Alice said thoughtfully, "Edd, are you certain you put the draft in your wallet? Might you have tucked it away somewhere else, meaning to put it in your wallet later, and then forgotten?"

"I don't think so, Allie, and anyway, my trunk is back at your folks' house," Edd said.

"Well, you have your valise, maybe it's in there," she persisted.

Finally, to please her, Edd sorted through his clothing, emptying the valise and making a thorough search. Then he began to riffle though the pockets of the two pairs of pants and an old jacket he had brought along. When he came to the jacket, he checked the outer pockets, then slipped his hand into a pocket in the lining and felt his fingers close around a crinkle of paper. He pulled out an envelope, looked inside, and there was the three-hundred-dollar draft. Wordlessly he held it out to Alice, and they both sank speechlessly onto the room's settee. Waves of profound relief rolled through Edd and he hugged Alice close to him.

"I guess you showed your forgetful husband a thing or two, Mrs. Yoder," he said teasingly, when he could speak. "And I guess we'll go to Livesay's Lumberyard tomorrow and pick out our house plan, for sure!"

That evening, after a pleasant dinner in the hotel dining room, Edd sat down at a small desk in the lobby and wrote several brief letters. The first was to his bank in Kenmare, letting them know that he had recovered the draft and that they could reach him in care of his wife's parents at Hubbard, Oregon. The second and third letters were to Aunt Mattie Kauffman in Dakota and to his family in Ohio, telling them of his marriage to Alice. As he wrote the words *I am married*, the occasional feelings of unreality that had plagued him ever since he left Dakota were swept away and he breathed a fervent prayer of thanks for his good fortune. The woman waiting for him in the room upstairs was more than a dream realized; she was a warm, intelligent, vivacious, and utterly lovable companion who trusted him enough to give her heart into his keeping. Once again, he vowed to be worthy of that trust.

STEALING A MARCH

When their honeymoon was over and Edd and Alice returned to her parent's home, letters of congratulations from Aunt Mattie and Edd's parents awaited them. Two letters also had arrived from the bank in Kenmare. The first, written the day of Edd's telegram, assured him that they would stop payment on the draft. The second letter acknowledged Edd's correspondence that he had recovered the draft and stated that the bank would now honor the check. The letter ended on a personal note and Edd chuckled as he read:

I think, Edd, that you stole a march on some of your friends; however, accept my heartiest congratulations [on your marriage].
Very truly yours,
George A. Trzcinski, Assistant Cashier

*As Edd begins to achieve success in his new community,
his life takes an unexpected turn.*

CHAPTER 27: Chosen by Lot

IN THE NEW YEAR, EDD AND ALICE chose furnishings for the large room they would occupy at the Troyer homestead while they were building their own house. A bed, washstand, two dressers, a wardrobe, and two comfortable chairs filled their cozy retreat and formed the nucleus of furnishings for their new home. As soon as they were settled, they began the traditional round of visits to relatives and close friends.

The newlyweds spent a few nights with each family they called upon, usually returning to Alice's parents' house for the weekend. These social calls, which continued for several weeks, introduced Edd to Alice's family and members of the community — especially other young married couples — and provided an opportunity for the hosts to give the newlyweds gifts. Useful items such as cooking utensils, tools, kerosene lamps, linens, and quilts were soon added to the Yoder's growing store of household goods.

In February, when a spell of warm spring weather laid its beneficent hand across the Valley, Edd prepared the building site for their new home. Because his woodworking skills were rudimentary, Edd agreed to exchange labor with several experienced carpenters in the community, and slowly the little house took shape. A thick stand of fir and deciduous trees sheltered the five-room dwelling to the south and west, and Edd planted a grove of cedar saplings between the house and the Zion Church building, which sat on a knoll to the north. Rock Creek bordered the property to the east, and in the front yard spring water bubbled abundantly from the mossy ground and trickled downhill to the creek.

The front door of the little house opened directly into a large living room. To the right, another door led to a dining room with a kitchen behind it. Two bedrooms were situated to the left of the living room and a long screened porch ran the length of the house in back. A woodshed reposed handily outside the back kitchen door, with an outhouse behind it, and a small barn stood down the slope to the south.

The trees wore autumn cloaks of red and gold before Edd and Alice moved into their new home. After nearly a year of living with Alice's parents and working for various neighbors to pay for labor and materials, Edd's relief at being independent and on his own farm again kept him doggedly working the land until winter rains turned the ground into a soggy sponge. A good part of the rolling property was in pasture, with lowlands that could be flooded by Rock Creek in years of heavy rainfall, making it difficult to plant a spring crop. So Edd decided to raise cows, hogs, and sheep. He attended several fall auctions to buy the few animals that would form the base of his herds and provide him and Alice with meat and milk.

Alice delighted in making a home of her own, away from her beloved but exacting parents' watchful eyes. The sparsely furnished house was easy to care for, but the daily chores of cooking, canning fruit and vegetables, sewing and washing clothes, starting a flock of chickens, and helping Edd prepare a large garden plot for spring planting filled her days to bursting.

True to his promise, Edd became a member of the Zion Mennonite Church, where his gift of oratory and wealth of pioneering stories soon made him a favorite with the younger members. Observing Edd's popularity with children as well as their parents, Bishop Troyer asked Edd to teach a Sunday School class and Edd readily agreed. When the young people's attendance blossomed, the church members elected Edd Sunday School Superintendent. So the winter and spring passed quickly and happily, generating in Edd a constant thankfulness. Days filled with rewarding work, a growing regard within the church and community, and the pleasure of making a home with Alice were the source of blessed calm that would keep him anchored in the storm of events that were about to roll over him, forever altering the shape of his life.

Early in the summer of 1911, Alice began feeling unwell, and by the end of June she was sure that she was going to have a baby. Pleased but somewhat overwhelmed by the news, Edd felt the gravity of becoming a father settle heavily on his thirty-year-old shoulders. As a child, and again as a young adult, Edd had vowed that his own children would never know the physical and emotional hardships he had endured, and now that test was upon him. But an even greater test was about to unfold.

Sunday, August 27, saw the Amish–Mennonite community

sweltering in a late-summer heat wave. In a pew on the women's side of the Zion church house, a three-months-pregnant Alice shifted uncomfortably and applied her fan vigorously to her flushed face. Her wedding dress, which she wore on Sundays as was traditional during the first year or so of marriage, felt unpleasantly tight.

I'll have to finish making my new winter dress quickly, she thought, even if we are still having summer weather.

Alice sighed and leaned heavily into the corner of the hard wooden pew. Today was Communion Sunday, which usually made the service longer, and after communion a new minister was to be chosen by lot. It would be midafternoon before she could get out of her too-tight dress and rest in the shady, north-facing front bedroom of the little house in the woods, Alice thought. She swallowed a wave of nausea and prayed that she wouldn't have to call attention to herself by leaving early.

Mercifully, her father's sermon was brief, and after the communion bread and grape juice had been passed down the long rows of benches and all church members had partaken, the congregation filed to the back of the church and paired off, men with men, women with women, to perform the solemn rite of foot washing. As the men finished communion, one by one they stepped downstairs to the basement, where Deacon Chris Yoder and Bishop Troyer sat before a wooden table, and cast their vote for the member they felt should be the next minister. After the men voted, the women took their turns. Deacon Yoder wrote down the name of each nominee and added marks after the names for each additional vote.

CHOSEN BY LOT

When all votes had been cast and counted, those men who had received less than three votes were dropped from the list, leaving four names. On a scrap of plain paper, Bishop Troyer slowly penned the words from Acts 1:26: "And they gave forth their lots; and the lot fell on Mathias: and he was numbered with the eleven Apostles." The bishop selected four, similarly worn hymnbooks from a stack on the table and placed the paper inside the front cover of one of them. Then he and Deacon Yoder climbed the stairs to the main floor, where congregation members had reseated themselves to await the outcome.

Bishop Troyer paced solemnly to the front of the church and placed the four hymnbooks in a row on the communion table in front of the pulpit. He asked the congregation to pray that God's will be done in selecting the new minister of Zion.

"I will now call the names of four men who have been nominated to serve," Amos said, when the prayer concluded. "As I call your name, will each man please come before the assembly and choose a hymnbook."

The third name he called was Edd Yoder.

Alice gave an involuntary start and pushed herself up straighter on the unyielding bench, her physical discomfort momentarily forgotten. She held her breath and looked over at Edd as he rose from his seat on the men's side of the church, quietly made his way to the front of the room, and chose a book. When all four men stood facing the congregation, the bishop walked down the row, taking the book from each man in turn and opening it. When he reached Edd, he paused a moment, and the father- and son-in-law exchanged a brief, sober glance. Amos reached out, took the hymnbook from Edd's hand and opened it. Then he placed his hand on Edd's shoulder and turned to the congregation.

"Today the lot falls on Brother Edd Yoder," he announced. "May God bless you as you go forward in His service."

Overcome, Edd stood in stunned silence, his head bowed.

In the space of a few seconds, a dozen scenes from childhood and youth flashed through his head: the lonely little boy outside the family circle; an even lonelier young man, ostracized for his shabby clothing, diffident manner, and lack of familial status; the hard, grinding years of making his own way — then, too, he remembered the sensation of his mother's hand on his shoulder in the rough saloon in Bemidji and Aunt Fanny's voice as she told him, "Your mother prayed that God would keep you always in the hollow of His hand."

Eyes locked on her husband's still figure, Alice felt a shock wave roll through her body as her father spoke the fateful words of election. For a frozen moment, her brain refused to accept what her ears had heard.

No, no, it cannot be true, she thought in near desperation. *Marrying Edd freed me from twenty-one years of being a bishop's daughter. How can I possibly be a minister's wife?*

But at last Edd lifted his head, and his blue eyes were poignantly clear as he looked at the men and women of the Zion congregation.

"Remember me in your prayers," he said.

CHAPTER 28: Birth and Death

DOCTOR SCHOOR'S SHINING BLACK BUGGY rolled swiftly down the lane and came to a halt in front of the Yoder's little house. Edd burst through the front door, crossed the porch in two strides, and reached for the horse's bridle. He tried to speak calmly to avoid startling the horse, but his face looked ghostly in the twilight and sweat beaded his forehead.

"She's in a lot of pain, Doc," Edd said, rubbing his free hand across his eyes, "and I don't know what to do for her."

"Now Edd, women go through childbirth all the time and pain is a natural part of it; she'll be better by and by. Have you fetched her mother?" Dr. Schoor enquired.

"I was afraid to leave Alice, even for a minute, but I'll go now that you're here," Edd said. He ushered the doctor into the living room, where Alice lay on her back on a long library table padded with several layers of blankets. As the men came through the door, Alice jerked and cried out as another hard contraction seized her body.

"How long has she been having contractions," the doctor asked.

"They started at about two o'clock this afternoon," Edd said. "And they're close together now."

The doctor glanced at his pocket watch. "About three hours in labor then," he noted. "If you'll go after her mother, I think it won't be long now."

Edd left the room gratefully, not stopping even for his jacket, and ran through the February evening mist across the fields to the big white farmhouse. He pounded on the door and waited impatiently for it to open. Suddenly Amos stood in the doorway, framed in the lamplight spilling from the door.

"From the looks of you, Alice's time is near," Amos said, as he surveyed Edd's disheveled appearance. "Come in, son, and we'll get Mother Troyer."

The men found Delilah in the pantry putting jars of herbs into a cloth bag. She caught up a handful of soft old cotton rags and stuffed them into the bag, too, tied the top shut with a piece of string, and bustled into the kitchen, shooing the men ahead of her toward the front hall.

"How is Alice doing?" she asked, as she drew her heavy cloak over her long dark dress and white apron and fastened it snugly down the front.

"She's having a difficult time; I would have come before, but I was afraid to leave her." Edd gasped, "Chauncey Kropf stopped by and I sent him for Doc Schoor. The doctor's with her now."

Edd and Delilah hurried back across the fields, but they needn't have rushed, for the hours ticked by as Edd paced back and forth in front of the little house, listening to Alice cry out. As her cries became weaker, Edd prayed harder than he'd ever prayed in his life. Long after the evening mealtime had passed unnoticed, Delilah came to the door.

BIRTH AND DEATH

"Edd, come in now," Delilah said softly. "She's losing ground and she needs you to help her rally and push that baby out."

Edd wiped his damp face on his handkerchief and came quietly into the room. Alice lay limply on the table, her knees drawn up, her silence more disturbing to him than her cries. When Edd grasped her hand it was nerveless with exhaustion, but he folded her cold fingers within his warm ones and spoke as calmly as he could.

"Allie, you must try very hard now, the baby needs to be born soon," he said.

"I can't Edd, oh, I can't," Alice gasped, breathing shallowly.

Edd's voice firmed and he gave her hand a little shake. "Alice, my dear, you can do this, for me and for our baby. I'm going to take both your hands and I want you to hold onto me as hard as you can and *push!*"

Alice gathered her remaining strength and locked her fingers around Edd's, although at first her touch was so light that his heart seemed to stop beating. Slowly she braced herself and her grip tightened as she put every ounce of her remaining energy into a final effort. A harsh scream ripped from her throat as a gush of blood spurted across the room and upward to the ceiling and the baby emerged into Dr. Schoor's waiting hands.

Delilah quickly took the crying infant and began to wipe it clean while the doctor worked over Alice. Unnoticed for the moment, Edd dropped to the wooden floor and put his head in his hands.

"It's a boy, Edd," Delilah said as she swaddled the baby in soft cloths. But he sat, dazed, his strength drained away, his muscles suddenly as limp as Alice's.

Later, when Edd and the doctor had moved a nearly lifeless Alice to the bed, tucked the baby in beside her, and the doctor had gone away, Edd could think only that she must never go through such agony again. He sat by the bed as Delilah bustled around the little house, clearing away all traces of the ordeal and preparing food for herself and Edd, and he prayed even more fervently than he had a few hours before, as though the very strength of his concentration would keep her alive. His thoughts drifted again and again to his little sister Pheba Ellen, who had died of typhoid exactly one month earlier. Only twenty years old, Pheba was just a little younger than Alice, and Edd thought, not for the first time, how quickly life's fragile flame could be snuffed out. When Delilah brought him a plate of food, he choked down a few bites without tasting them and continued his anxious vigil as the darkness slowly gave way to dawn.

Although she was young and strong, Alice's recovery took several weeks. For days she lay flat and still, unable to move from side to side without agonizing pain from her strained and knotted muscles. As soon as she felt well enough, however, she and Edd discussed what they should name the baby.

"You had such a hard time birthing him, I think you ought to choose his name," Edd told her. But Alice had other ideas.

"We'll have other babies, but he's the first son, and I want you to name him," she said emphatically.

"Well then, I'd like to name him after my uncle, Paul Emmons Whitmer, who teaches bible study at Goshen College," Edd said.

BIRTH AND DEATH

"I have the deepest respect for that great man, and if our son turns out half so well as Uncle Paul, I will be well pleased." So it was settled, and little Paul Emmons quickly became the center of his parents' lives.

But even as he shouldered the responsibilities of providing for his wife and child, Edd increasingly was called to care for his larger family, the religious community he had been chosen to serve. Inevitably, as time went on, the second responsibility would begin to overshadow the first.

The Zion Mennonite Church was built in 1898. The congregation originally was known as the Fir Grove meeting when it met in a structure near Woodburn. When members built the new church building just east of Hubbard, the men who were roofing the structure were singing, "Who will go along with me to Zion?" Whereupon Emmanual Kenagy suggested they name the new church building Zion. An addition was built onto the structure as the congregation grew, and in 1957 a new and much larger building was constructed.

CHAPTER 29: A Preacher's Way

SLEET RATTLED AGAINST THE WINDOWS, partially awakening Edd, who burrowed deeper into the bedclothes to shut out the near-freezing night air. Before he could lapse back into oblivion, however, the thud of hoof beats brought him fully awake. He slipped out of bed, tucking the quilts more snugly around Alice. As he pulled on his overalls, a heavy knock sounded on the front door. Edd closed the bedroom door quietly behind him and crossed to the front door, his bare feet shrinking away from the frosty nip of the cold wooden floorboards.

"It's Abraham Schrock, Mr. Yoder; I live along the Barlow Road," a distraught voice answered Edd's greeting. "I've come about my missus and my little girl; they're both sick with the typhoid and I don't know if they'll live through the night; the doctor says he's done all he can. Won't you please come and pray for them?"

"Of course, of course, give me a few moments to saddle my horse and I'll be right along after you," Edd promised.

Edd closed the door and slipped back into the bedroom to finish dressing, but quiet as he was, Alice heard him and asked, softly so as not to wake little Paul, "Who was at the door, Edd?"

"The Schrocks are down with typhoid and the crisis has come;

they want me to come pray with them," Edd told her.

No stranger to such calls, which had come at all hours in the Troyer household, Alice knew better than to protest his going out into the stormy March night. Tossing back the covers, she swung her feet out of bed and reached for her heavy woolen wrapper.

"Stop back by the house when you have Nell saddled and I'll have something hot ready for you," she said.

Bundled well against the bone-numbing cold, Edd hurried to the barn to ready his horse while Alice stirred up the embers in the cookstove and added a pile of kindling to make a quick, hot fire. She poured milk into a pan and used a paring knife to shave thin strips from a small bar of chocolate that she'd been saving for a treat. While the milk was heating and the chocolate melting, she spread bacon drippings on slices of homemade bread and made a rough sandwich. The rich smells of hot chocolate and bacon grease made her stomach growl, but she ignored her hunger and poured every sweet drop of the hot liquid into a heavy ironstone mug. She had the hot chocolate and the bacon dripping sandwich ready when Edd led the horse around the front of the house and looped its reins over the porch railing.

"Allie, you'll catch your death of pneumonia standing there in the cold," Edd admonished, "and not six weeks since the baby was born!"

Alice suppressed a shiver and smiled as she handed him the food. "I'm fine, Edd, and I don't have to ride five miles in this weather," she said gently. "Here, eat a few bites and drink your chocolate, you may not get anything more to put in your stomach for quite a while."

A PREACHER'S WAY

Not more than five minutes later, Edd set the empty mug on the porch, untied Nell, and swung into the saddle. As he turned the mare toward the road, he saw Alice holding baby Paul and waving goodbye from the front bedroom window. He turned his face into the stinging sleet and urged Nell to a trot.

Late the next morning, Edd rode into the barnyard, horse and rider both looking the worse for wear. Wearily he unsaddled Nell, rubbed the mare down, and made sure that she was clean, dry, and fed before he walked slowly up the knoll to the house, exhaustion evident in every step. The spring storm had passed in the night and the air snapped clear and cold. March had gone out like a lion, taking Abe Schrock's wife, Hannah, with it. The little girl still lived, Edd told Alice, as she bustled around the kitchen putting a hot meal on the table, but her recovery was far from certain.

That evening another knock on the door called Edd to the bedside of yet another typhoid sufferer, and for a week or more it seemed to Alice that he was away more often than he was home. Twice a day when he was gone, Alice bundled baby Paul into a basket and carried him to the barn with her to feed and water their other horse and the cow. Their few head of sheep were grazing in the pasture and the cow hadn't dropped its calf yet so didn't need milking, but Alice was still recovering from Paul's birth and moved slowly about the house and farmyard. She didn't complain — what good would it have done! — but she was relieved when Edd was home again to do the chores.

Now, in the evenings, Edd spent much of his time reading,

studying his Bible, and thinking about sermon topics. Amish–Mennonite congregations typically had several preachers in addition to the bishop and deacon, but Edd was the only minister at Zion, so he preached most Sundays. Although he had become a practiced orator during his years in North Dakota, guiding the spiritual lives of his fellow parishioners proved far more daunting than discoursing on an abstract topic to entertain an audience. Nonetheless, Edd knew how to tell a story and how to keep his listeners' attention, so over time he became known as a "story preacher," who used dramatic experiences from his own life and that of others to illuminate each spiritual lesson.

Like many converts who came late to religious practice, Edd appreciated how his conversion had changed his life for the better in so many ways. His first ringing words from the pulpit each Sunday were, "Thank God for salvation!"

Ministers received no pay for their services, so Edd continued to increase his herds of livestock. He also planted a few acres in berries, which grew well in Oregon's temperate climate. Edd and Alice picked the wild blackberries that clustered thickly along Rock Creek and sold them at the general store in Hubbard. Still, money was tight, and Edd labored for other farmers whenever he could.

The first annual land payment from his Dakota farm had arrived the previous December and Edd had used the money to purchase the handful of sheep that now grazed his lush pasture. He continued to lease his eighty Dakota acres on shares, so any income from that property depended on the quality and quantity of the year's crop. In the back of Edd's mind rested the thought that if he couldn't make a go of farming in Oregon, he could always take Alice and the baby and go back to North Dakota. No need to mention the idea to Alice, but it was good for a man to have a backup plan just in case.

CHAPTER 30: Rumors of War

Late in the fall of 1912, Alice realized that she was again pregnant. Little Paul was only eight months old and still required a large share of her time and attention, but Alice calculated that he would be almost a year and a half old when the new baby came. When she told Edd the news, however, his concern was evident.

"I'm happy about the baby, of course," Edd told her, "but after what you went through having Paul, I'm afraid for you. This time you must have the baby in the hospital," he finished determinedly.

"Oh Edd, how can we afford the hospital, it's much too expensive," Alice cried.

"You mustn't worry, Alice, we'll use the next Dakota land payment if we have to," Edd said. Privately his heart sank a little as he began to realize that his growing family could use that land payment a dozen times over. Well, it will simply take a little longer to build up the farm, he thought; Alice's and the baby's health are the most important considerations.

On July 12, 1913, Alice gave birth to a baby girl. The delivery was easier this time and Alice was able to go home after only a few days in the hospital. Feeling blessed and thankful, Edd and Alice named the baby Charity Loretta Rebecca, because Charity means *love*, Edd reminded Alice, as he quoted from I Corinthians: "Faith, hope, and charity, and the greatest of these is charity."

Edd worked hard to support his growing family, but cash money was always scarce; nonetheless, Edd bought a newspaper whenever he could to keep abreast of local and world news. He also studied theology in the evenings and sometimes far into the night, determined to give himself the equivalent of a college education so that he could acquit himself well as a minister and spiritual advisor. Exhausted by physical labor, at day's end Edd's back ached too badly for him to stand or sit, so he read and studied while lying on the living room floor. Sometimes, too, intense migraine headaches racked his body. At such times Edd soaked his feet in very hot water while Alice applied compresses to his head and neck, but he had far too much to do to take to his bed. During one such bout, Edd speculated to Alice about the source of his migraines.

"When I was only a boy," he told Alice, "I was playing baseball with the other children and my position was catcher. A little girl came up to bat and she was so excited, she swung hard and missed the ball by a mile, but the bat flew out of her hand and hit me in the side of the head instead. It cracked my head open and I was unconscious for quite some time. The surgeon who patched me up used a thin steel plate to reinforce the place where my skull bone shattered. I often think that my old head injury is the reason I have such headaches now," he added.

"Maybe so," Alice replied, as she held a hot compress to the back of Edd's neck, "but I think having too many irons in the fire doesn't help matters."

In the summer of 1914, newspapers chronicled the assassination of Archduke Ferdinand and the subsequent events that led Europe inexorably into war. By late summer, Germany had invaded Belgium, causing Great Britain in turn to declare war on Germany. As the war spread, speculation grew as to whether the United States would get involved. If it did, conscription seemed inevitable. Canada, a British colony, was already involved in the war, and Mennonites in that country were forced to deal with the draft issue immediately.

From the Mennonite church's beginnings in sixteenth-century Anabaptism, its leaders had defined its position as one of nonresistance based on the biblical injunction to "resist not evil." Founder Menno Simons believed that turning the other cheek, no matter how seriously one was reviled or injured, even unto death, was an essential article of faith. "Our weapons are not swords and spears, but patience, silence and hope, and the Word of God," Simons wrote. "With these we must maintain our cause and defend it."

Early preacher and teacher Jacob Ammons' message was much the same. Ammons' followers became known as Amish, while Simons' followers were called Menists or Mennonites. Ultimately the peace-loving Amish and Mennonites flowed together into a river of believers that encompassed the strictest practitioners, known as Old Order Amish, through increasingly liberal (though still conservative by the world's standards) tiers of Amish, Amish–Mennonites, (Old) Mennonites, and thence to the most liberal group, General Conference Mennonites.

For several hundred years, members of those "peace churches" had emigrated as necessary to countries such as Russia, the Netherlands, Switzerland, and finally to America, because the rulers of those countries initially promised them exemption from military service. The Civil War brought a repeal of such promises in the United States, and young Mennonite men were forced to choose between abandoning their principles of faith, fleeing to Canada, or paying as much as one thousand dollars to buy their freedom from conscription. The church paid the exemption for those who held firm and refused to bear arms; later those men gave back a specified amount of time and labor to the congregation to repay the debt.

In lesser wars, such as the War of 1812, the Mexican War, and the Spanish-American War, service was voluntary. But now, once again, Mennonites feared that their men and boys could face imprisonment or worse if they refused to fight, and the various churches began to debate and define what their response would be. Quakers, Hutterites, Dunkards, and other groups also struggled to define their position concerning military service. Unfortunately, almost as many shades of compliance and noncompliance were to emerge as there were groups of pacifists, and the lack of a unified voice only added to the confusion.

In 1915, the General Conference Mennonites scheduled a meeting near Archibold, Ohio, to hammer out a consensus position concerning warfare. Edd had been closely following news of the war and the debate among church leaders, so when the conference was announced in the church paper, he immediately decided to attend. He wanted to hear the discussions and conclusions firsthand, for he knew that many young men in the community would look to him for guidance if America entered the war. Then, too, he had not seen his aging parents nor his stepbrothers and stepsisters for five years, and the trip to Ohio would allow him to do so. Their third child was due at the end of June, but Alice begged Edd to take her and the children along, and at last he agreed. "But only if you have the baby well before the trip and are fully recovered," he admonished.

Edd's father, Ezra B. Yoder, left, and his uncle, David B. Ezra was known as a peacemaker in the church.

CHAPTER 31: Taking a Stand

EARLY IN AUGUST, the Yoder family boarded a train to Ohio with a stop in North Dakota planned en route. Three-year-old Paul and two-year-old Charity — nicknamed Taggly because she insisted on following her Papa everywhere on her unsteady little legs — gripped their father's hands while Alice carried the month-old baby, Lois Mae Etta. Lois had arrived on July 6, barely in time to allow her mother to prepare for the journey. Alice still hadn't fully recovered her strength, but she hid her tiredness from Edd and coped as well as she could with the children's antics.

Paul and Charity wriggled excitedly on the plush seats of the Pullman car. Papa had said that they would sleep on the train in those berths that looked like cozy little playhouses, and at the end of the long journey they would meet a new-to-them grandpa and grandma. Inquisitively, the children poked their little fingers into everything they could reach, but their high spirits were soon dampened when little Paul soundly pinched his finger trying to open the intriguing, metal-frame window in the upper berth. He required much comforting and cosseting to stop his wails, which kept the whole family awake for more than an hour, even though Alice applied cold compresses to his now very blue and purple fingertip. Baby Lois howled, too, in sympathy, but Charity only sat big-eyed in the lower berth and observed the commotion. The incident sobered the children, and for the remainder of the trip east they were quiet and well behaved.

The family broke their journey on the North Dakota prairies, where they visited Aunt Mattie Kauffman; her sons Lee, Dan, and Willie; and their sister Fannie Kauffman Morningstar and husband Lewis. Discouraged by several years of poor crops, some of the cousins had moved on to try their luck elsewhere, but a few second cousins remained. Lee's teenage sons, Milo and Archie, were looking for land to farm, and Edd agreed to let them work his eighty acres near Kenmare on shares while they tried to save enough money to buy the property outright.

One day while Edd and Alice were visiting with the elder Kauffmans, the youngsters took Paul and Charity outdoors to play. Eventually the children ended up in the turnip field, where they took turns pulling turnips to see who could find the biggest root. One turnip was so large and odd-shaped it looked like a baby pig, which inspired the children to play at pig butchering. The "pig" was decapitated, then cut in crisp slices and eaten for a snack.

From Kenmare, the Ohio-bound train wound through Canada and along the northern shore of Lake Superior, and for the first time the Yoders saw men in uniform. Canadian troops were riding the rails east to join the battle overseas, and women of all ages lined the station platforms to wave goodbye. As the train rolled slowly through one of the towns, Edd noticed several stockades, or

TAKING A STAND

work camps, hastily built to house German prisoners of war. The family also saw troops drilling and marching as the train steamed past. Those chilling sights brought home the dreadfulness and solemnity of war as no printed words could do.

Edd's father met them at the station in West Liberty, Ohio. Now in his sixty-first year, Ezra Yoder was quieter than Edd remembered, and he moved more slowly, but a jolly laugh still occasionally rang out from Ezra's heavily bearded face and his eyes twinkled as he bent his burly frame to meet his grandchildren.

"They're fine-looking youngsters," he said to Edd, "and they've come along in good time. I was beginning to think I might not live to see grandchildren from you," he joked.

As Ezra drove the two-seater buggy along the lane leading to the homestead, Edd noticed how prosperous the farm looked, its trimly painted buildings sheltered by tall maples and oaks; its well-tilled fields rich with bountiful crops of oats, corn, and sorghum; and it's pastures dotted with sleek cattle and hogs. Grandmother Lydia greeted them from the open doorway of the two-storey farmhouse, a large white apron covering much of her dark gray calico dress sprigged with tiny blue flowers. A white lawn cap covered her snowy hair. She hugged Edd and Alice warmly and kissed each of the children, then she led the way upstairs to help them get settled before dinner.

Edd's sisters Fannie and Anna still lived at home, and the young women quickly took charge of the children to allow Alice, who was still feeling the effects of recent childbirth, some much-needed rest. Fannie stood little Charity upon the seat of a wooden kitchen chair to watch as she prepared beef stew for dinner, but when Fannie began to chop onions, Charity rubbed her eyes and started to cry.

"Oh, they burn, they burn," she sobbed, rubbing vigorously, which only increased her discomfort.

Grandmother Yoder bustled into the kitchen when she heard Charity crying. She lifted Charity off the chair, wiped the little girl's eyes with a soft handkerchief, and handed her a cookie to distract her from her discomfort. Charity sat on her grandmother's lap, munched her cookie, and watched the meal preparations from a safe distance. When the stew was simmering in a large pot on the black cast-iron cook stove, Grandmother led Paul and Charity into the parlor and opened the door of a bow-front curio cabinet.

"I have a present for each of you," she told them. "You can take these upstairs to your mother to keep them safe for you until you are home again," and she handed each child a small bisque vase.

On one side of Paul's vase a boy stood holding a fishing rod, and on the side of Charity's vase a little girl had just lifted a jug of water from the well. The children clutched the softly painted ceramic figurines in open-mouthed wonder, their little fingers examining each detail, then Paul remembered his manners and said "thank you" and Charity echoed him.

While Edd attended the Mennonite General Conference, Alice rested and visited with Edd's family and the children roamed the farm under their grandparents' and aunts' watchful eyes. For

TAKING A STAND

three days Edd listened as the Conference attendees debated the church's position on warfare. At the end of that time they reaffirmed a nonresistant stance, the first words of which were: "We believe that in the light of the life and teaching of Christ and the apostles, no Christian should engage in carnal warfare under any circumstances nor for any cause."

The brief statement went on to say that when the government participated in war, Mennonites should pray for their rulers, but should be willing to suffer affliction and persecution themselves rather than inflict violence on others. "Brethren drafted for military service should state their position on nonresistance meekly but unhesitatingly, get relieved if that is possible, but if forced by violence into the army, should suffer themselves to be imprisoned or court-martialed rather than do anything which could in any way result in the loss of life at their hands." A committee also wrote letters to President Wilson and Canada's Premier Gordon affirming the position of General Conference members in the United States, Canada, and India and stating that "[we] believe it to be the Christian duty of our people to refrain from taking up arms."

That the committee's stance would be willfully at odds with the United States' intent to defend itself from perceived threats abroad was a given, and along with members of the Mennonite and Amish churches, the Quakers, the Brethren, and various other religious bodies, Edd was soon to find himself embroiled in a conflict that pitted the power and might of the U.S. military against the nonresistant beliefs of the peace churches.

**HEADQUARTERS
91st INFANTRY DIVISION
CAMP LEWIS
AMERICAN LAKE, WASH.**

Memorandum: July 8, 1918.

TO WHOM IT MAY CONCERN:

    1. The Bearer, Edward Z. Yoder, representing the Mennonite Church will be permitted to interview the following men of this command.

    2. It is understood that at all times during the interview a commissioned officer shall be present.

Alvin D. Hamilton,
   37th Co., 10th Bn.,
     166th Depot Brigade.
Elmer H. Schultz, 46th Co.,
     166th Depot Brigade.
David Y. Schrock.
Frank J. Hastetler
Paul Snyder
Percy Conrad
Moses D. Miller.

    (Hugo K. Visscher),
    1st Lieutenant, Inf.R.C.,
    Camp Intelligence Section

**CAMP HEADQUARTERS
CAMP LEWIS
AMERICAN LAKE, WASH.**

Memorandum for:

Edward Z. Yoder a minister of the Mennonite faith, has permission to visit such members of this sect as he may desire to interview.

Henry C. Breck
1st Lt. Inf. R.C.

Permits were required for ministers to visit conscientious objectors held at army training camps during World War I. Even with a permit, visitation was not guaranteed.

CHAPTER 32: Mennonites and War

IN 1917, GERMANY VIOLATED its pledge to suspend submarine warfare in the North Atlantic and Mediterranean oceans and attempted to engage Mexico as an ally, leading President Woodrow Wilson to ask Congress for a declaration of war. On April 6, the United States of America joined France, Britain, Russia, Italy, Romania, and Japan (the Allies) in the war against Germany, Austria-Hungary, Bulgaria, and the Ottoman Empire (the Central Powers).

Six weeks later, on May 18, the U.S. Congress passed the Selective Service Act, which allowed the government to draft Americans into military service. Not since the Civil War had military conscription been a reality in the United States. And once again, Amish and Mennonites, as well as members of sects such as the Quakers and the Brethren, found themselves living in a country where promises of freedom from conscription were now called into question.

In the midst of the country's run-up to war, Alice gave birth to the family's fourth child: a baby boy who was named after his father, Edward Z. Little Eddy arrived on April 23, as a long cold winter was finally giving way to spring, but his arrival was somewhat overshadowed by the larger events going on around him.

It had been an especially hard winter for Alice because Edd was working away from home six days a week, and she had been left alone to care for three children and the family's livestock during the latter part of her pregnancy. Edd had gotten work at a sawmill owned by local entrepreneur Jake Egli. Because the sawmill was too far from home to go back and forth every day by horse and buggy, Jake picked Edd up early every Monday morning in his automobile and returned him to his family on Saturday evening. Jake was a good friend as well as a considerate boss, and often he sent oranges or bananas home with Edd as treats for the children. Nevertheless, it was difficult for the family to be separated during the week.

Edd stayed in a bunkhouse at the mill where, after an indifferent evening meal, he spent most evenings reading, studying, and preparing a sermon for the coming Sunday. When he arrived home on Saturday night, he must put the finishing touches on his sermon for the next day and check on his livestock. Sunday was spent preaching and tending to the needs of his congregation. At times, his life seemed nearly impossible to manage, but there was no choice: the position of pastor was unpaid and Edd had a growing family to support.

The burden was equally heavy on Alice, who must milk the cows that were fresh twice a day, keep the stock troughs filled with water, and throw down hay for the cows and sheep, as well as take care of the children and all the domestic chores. Occasionally one of her younger sisters would stop in for an hour or two to help, but mostly Alice found she had to rely on young

MENNONITES AND WAR

Paul to help her carry the milk pails, feed the stock, and watch out for the younger children while she worked.

Alice missed Edd terribly; this was the first time they had been apart for any length of time since they were married. Sometimes after the children were asleep Alice sat in her rocking chair by the wood burning stove and cried a little as she mended the children's clothes. But most of the time she was so exhausted by day's end that she went to bed not long after the children.

Spring and the new baby, which brought Edd home for a few weeks, would have been most welcome had it not been for the uncertainties of a world at war. By now, feeling was running high against all things German, and the Amish–Mennonite community, many of whose members still spoke German at home, was beginning to be a target of those feelings. Moreover, Edd now needed to be available to counsel the young men of his congregation, who were certain to be called up in the draft.

The most liberal portion of the Amish–Mennonite continuum — the General Conference Mennonites — had endorsed "noncombatant service," which meant that draftees could accept military service "designed to support and to save life," such as work in hospitals or in a support role at the front. However the separate and more conservative community of believers known as the Mennonite Church, which Edd and Alice Yoder belonged to, believed that church members should choose the path of conscientious objection to any form of military participation and refuse to be conscripted into the military or wear military uniforms. The Mennonite Church's position was that "under no circumstance can [members] consent to service, either combatant or noncombatant, under the military arm of the government."

The slightly different positions of the two groups caused confusion, both among Mennonites and within the U.S. military, which generally viewed all Mennonites as unpatriotic slackers.

Every man who received a draft notice must appear before his local draft board to plead his case, but exemptions were arbitrary at the local level. Most of the men who objected on religious grounds were denied exemption due to local predjudices or uninformed interpretation of the Act. Even if one were not exempted from the draft, however, it was still possible to retain conscientious objector or noncombatant status. The Selective Service Act gave noncombatant status to members of well-established religious groups whose doctrines forbade participation in combat, but until 1918 there was no plan laid out for noncombatant service outside of the military. As a result, for the first year the United States was at war, twenty thousand men who had been granted conscientious objector status were sent to army training camps.

In the Pacific Northwest, where prejudice against German-speaking Americans was now at its height, Amish–Mennonite draftees were taken to army camps, where their clothing was taken from them and they were told they must put on uniforms and participate in military drills and training. If they refused, they were mistreated and abused in an attempt to wear them down and force compliance. Abuse took many forms, including withholding food; sleep deprevation; and stripping the men naked in cold weather and dousing them with freezing cold water, then scrubbing their bodies with brushes used to clean the latrines.

MENNONITES AND WAR

When they refused to train, men were stabbed in the legs with bayonets or put in unshaded fenced areas in the hot sun. In colder seasons, some were thrown naked into pits dug in the ground until they passed out from hypothermia. Strong in their faith, some men died rather than wear military uniforms and train for combat.

Mennonite ministers who tried to visit the men in training camps were actively disuaded from doing so. Often they were told that the person they had come to visit was not there or could not be located. Eventually, however, persistance was rewarded, and word of the mistreatment and abuses of conscientious objectors began to circulate. As news of the conditions in the camps reached Edd Yoder, he became determined to visit the training camps throughout Oregon, Washington, and Northern California to counsel and pray with the young men of the church, and to fight for decent treatment for them.

For each man he wanted to visit, Edd must have a permit signed by the commanding officer. Getting those permits often was a long, drawn-out process designed to discourage visitors.

In July 1918, Edd took the train to American Lake, Washington, to visit seven young Mennonite men at Camp Lewis. The men were Alvin D. Hamilton, Elmer H. Schultz, David Y. Schrock, Frank J. Hastetler, Paul Snyder, Percy Conrad, and Moses D. Miller. Edd was given access to all of the men except Elmer Schultz. Back and forth he walked across the camp all afternoon, from one office to another. In every office he was made to sit and wait: first no one would admit that Schultz was in camp, then they could not locate him, then the commanding officer was too busy to sign the permit. And so the day went by. Toward evening, Edd walked to the office of the commanding officer and told his assistant, "I'm going to wait right here until you let me see Elmer Schultz, even if it takes all night." Seeing Edd's determination, the CO finally told his assistant to take Edd to the young man. Schultz was imprisoned in a basement room with windows at ground level, and all day he had looked out his window and watched Edd walk back and forth across the camp, but had no way to get his attention.

While Edd was praying with and counseling Elmer, two guards came in and told Edd it was time to leave. "You go with us," one said. "We'll take you out the back way." When Edd asked why, he was told, "There are a group of ministers waiting for you out front who mean to make trouble for you." Those ministers were from churches that did not practice nonresistance and resented the fact that members of the peace churches refused to fight.

On a visit to a camp in Northern California, again one of the men Edd had come to see could not be located. Edd was shuttled from office to office with no success. Finally, as night fell, he decided to climb a tree to get a look at how the camp was laid out and see whether he could locate where the young man might be held. As he sat quietly in the tree, two guards passed nearby, laughing and talking to each other. "That slacker minister will never find who he's looking for," one said. "We've got that traitor down in the pit, and if that Yoder doesn't watch it, he'll end up down there with him." After the men were out of sight, Edd climbed down the tree and made for the gate.

That night, as Edd checked into his hotel room, the desk clerk called him aside. "There's a telegram here for you, sir," he said. In his room, Edd unfolded the yellow slip of paper, which contained a message from his brother-in-law, John Berkey.

Men waiting for you at Hubbard tomorrow. Continue on to Portland. Call and I will pick you up. John B.

On the one hand, it was hard for Edd to believe that his life might be in danger; on the other hand, he knew that John would not have spent money on a telegram unless he had good reason.

I will decide what to do when I get closer to home, Edd thought.

The next day, Edd felt increasingly uneasy as his train drew near the station at Hubbard. As his discomfort grew, Edd bowed his head in prayer. When he finally raised his head, he had made a decision: rather than embark at Hubbard, he would travel on to Portland. Just before the train came into the Hubbard station, Edd sequestered himself in the restroom and stayed there until he felt the coach moving again.

A short time later, the train steamed into Portland. Edd looked out the train window before he left the coach. Seeing nothing amiss, he stepped down onto the wooden platform, made his way into the station, and used the public telephone to call his brother-in-law.

"John, I took your advice and stopped in Portland, can you come and get me?" Edd asked.

"I'll be there as quickly as I can," John agreed. "I'll take a roundabout way."

Winter twilight was fast approaching as John and Edd traveled down the winding two-lane road toward home. As they drove through Hubbard on a street just west of the train station, a chilling sight met their eyes.

"That can't be what I think it is!" Edd exclaimed.

John gasped, nearly speechless with dismay. "It — it's a gallows," he said. "I had no idea they would go this far!"

"That Station Agent P— sold me a round-trip ticket when I left for the camp in Northern California and knew I was due back today from visiting the boys," Edd said. "He hates Germans, you know, and thinks all Mennonites are traitors or spies. I heard his son was killed overseas."

"We'd better get home as quickly as possible," he added. "I'm afraid for Allie and the children."

CHAPTER 33: Lynch Mob

NIGHT HAD FALLEN BY THE TIME John dropped Edd off at the little five-room house nestled in the woods. Alice was glad to see him home and reached up to embrace him, but as Edd hugged her tightly she saw at once that he was tense and troubled.

"What is it, Edd," she asked. "Did something happen on your trip to upset you?"

Edd evaded her questions for a few moments as he greeted the children and settled them back at the table to finish their supper of fried cornmeal mush and milk. Then he said, "Come into our bedroom for a moment, Allie, I have something I need to tell you."

"You know that there's bad feeling against the Germans in some of the local towns, we've talked about this before," he began. "It seems that my trips to visit the boys in the army training camps have not gone unnoticed, and a group of men were gathered at the Hubbard train station to accost me when I got off the train this afternoon. John heard what they were up to and sent me a telegram to go on through to Portland and he would pick me up. But when we drove through Hubbard on the way home, we saw that the men had erected a gallows. I hate to think that it was for me," he concluded, "but I don't know what else it could be for."

Alice was shocked and frightened, but managed to speak calmly as she asked, "Do you think they will come here when they don't see you get off the train? Are we in danger?"

"I don't know," Edd replied. "I'm afraid it might be so. But we have no weapons to defend ourselves. We will have to trust in God to protect us; to put a wall around us so that no one can harm us."

Alice thought for a moment. "The children have finished their supper; I'll bed them down here in the living room on the floor so we're all together and we can turn out all the lights," she suggested. "If anyone comes here, maybe they will think we're not at home."

Quickly Edd and Alice pulled quilts and comforters off the beds and made a comfortable pallet on the floor. Baby Edward was too young to understand what was happening, but five-year-old Paul, four-year-old Charity, and two-year-old Lois were at first excited to "camp" on the floor, and then sobered when they realized their parents were worried about something. Alice settled the three little ones into bed and sat down near them in the rocker with baby Edward, while Edd made sure the doors and windows were secured and blew out the lamps.

Exhausted, his back aching, Edd laid down on the floor next to the rocking chair and reached up for Alice's hand. Softly, Alice sang a hymn to coax the children to sleep. Then the couple began to pray, silently at first so as not to wake the little ones, then in lowered voices, first one, then the other, to keep their courage up as the hours passed. Neither felt able to go to sleep. Whatever came, they would face it awake and together.

The group of men waiting at the Hubbard train station became more and more agitated and impatient as the afternoon waned and turned to evening. When Edd didn't get off the late afternoon train, they decided to wait until the last passenger train of the evening went through around eight o'clock.

"Don't give up yet boys," Station Agent P— urged them. "He'll be along later for sure."

But the eight o'clock train came and went and Edd Yoder did not appear.

"Let's head over to the tavern and have a drink to warm us up, boys," one of the men suggested. "Then we'll decide what to do next. We may have to pay that Yoder a visit at home."

"I ain't hangin' no women and children," one of the men grumbled.

"If we hang the traitor, I'm sure his woman and kids will leave on their own," P— sneered.

After an hour or so spent in the tavern, the men were fueled with liquid courage and ready to carry out their plan. As they talked among themselves, boasting about ridding their town of Germans in general and Edd Yoder in particular, a man sitting at the end of the bar listened without comment. He soon finished his drink and quietly moved away from the bar and into the shadows, then slipped out the door and made for home. Once he reached the shelter of his handsome home in the nicest part of town, he made a single phone call to a well-known personage in the local judicial system. When the call was finished, he hung up the phone and ran his fingers through his hair until it stood up wildly.

"I've done all I can do," he muttered to himself, "it's in God's hands now."

At the tavern, the men had decided on their next move. One of them had gone home and returned with makeshift torches: thick pieces of wood dipped in tar, which they intended to use to light their way as they approached their target.

"I say we go to Yoder's house and tell him to come out or we'll go in after him," one of the men said, and the rest yelled agreement.

The men piled into a wagon and the driver whipped the reins over the horses' backs as the mob rolled out of town toward the little house tucked down in the woods near Zion Church. When they reached the church, the driver jumped down and tied the horses to a hitching post as the men tumbled out of the wagon. One pulled out some matches and lit the ends of the torches, then the men moved as one toward the little house.

When they got to a short picket fence that surrounded the front yard, the men stopped to catch their breath. Now that they were here at Edd's house, the reality of their actions and the possible consequences was setting in. But they'd come this far, and the mob mentality had long since kicked in: the men bolstered each other with muttered curses and epithets against the "heinies" and "traitors."

"The house is dark," one of the men observed, "do you think

they knew we were coming and ran?"

"They're probably cowards as well as traitors," another commented.

"I say we go up to the house and bang on the door," a third man said, and reached out his hand to open the gate. Before his hand could connect with the wooden pickets, however, he felt resistance; almost as though his hand had touched an invisible wall.

"What the —" he started to say, when he heard the sound of running footfalls coming down the path from the church.

As the men turned as one to look behind them, a young man burst out of the trees and moved quickly toward his father, who was one of the instigators of the ugly gathering.

"Father, wait," he puffed, out of breath. "A call — there was a call a little while ago from Judge —," the young man named a well-respected figure in the community. "He knows what's happening, and he said to tell you and the other men to leave Edd Yoder alone or there would be serious consequences," he gasped out the message.

The men looked at one another, waiting to see who would speak first, as Edd's fate shifted in the balance. The pause stretched out; the silence was grim.

The young man's father was the first to speak: "Ah hell," he swore, grimacing. "Come on boys, let's go. We'll get the traitor another time."

As the torch-carrying men moved back toward the church, the silence inside the little house was complete, but both Edd and Alice were on their knees praying next to the four little ones asleep on the pallet at their side.

All night they prayed, and as the first streaks of light paled the eastern sky, Edd got to his feet, wearily pulled on his jacket, and went out to care for the livestock. Equally weary, but calm and relieved to have made it through the night, Alice rose to begin preparing breakfast before the children began to stir. Outside in the early dawn twilight, the gate in the fence remained closed and the invisible wall that surrounded the little house remained firmly in place.

In later years when Edd talked with his children about that night, he always told them, "The Lord saved us."

CHAPTER 34: "We Have a Right"

AFTER A FEW DAYS AT HOME to reassure Alice, Edd took the train to Portland to speak with District Attorney Bert Haney about how the Mennonite boys were being treated in the camps. When he was ushered into the D.A.'s office the blond, cold-eyed Haney looked Edd over from his worn suit to his shabby shoes and waited impatiently for him to state his business.

Haney did not ask him to sit down, so Edd stood at ease on the deep red plush carpet and clasped his hands behind him as he surveyed the walnut paneled room, the shelves of leather-bound law books, and Haney himself, standing behind his massive desk wearing an expensive, well-cut suit. The contrast between the two men could not have been more marked, but Edd was not intimidated by his surroundings; he had been in luxurious settings before and worn such suits himself earlier in his life. Moreover, his reasons for being in that office were far more important than any exterior trappings, however resplendent.

As Edd began to recount how the young Mennonite men were being tortured, Haney's face grew redder and redder until finally he interrupted Edd with a shout:

"You people are traitors to this great country and deserve

everything you get," he yelled. "You come here for freedom and then refuse to fight for it! You lazy slackers let others die for you because you are afraid to fight!"

On and on Haney raved, pounding his fist on the desktop, never letting Edd get a word in, getting madder and madder until finally he shouted,

"What would you do if a German soldier stuck his bayonet through the belly of your pregnant wife? Would you fight then? Would you? Or would you turn yellow and run?"

Edd waited until Haney paused for breath and then he spoke quietly, "I don't know what I would do in such a situation," he said, "but I know we have a right to choose conscientious objection to this war and to be treated fairly. The president has given us that right. And that's all I'm asking for; that our young men receive the rights the president has promised us."

As the two men continued to talk, D.A. Haney reluctantly listened to what Edd had come to tell him about the foundations of Mennonite faith and why church members refused to participate in war. Haney listened closely when Edd recounted the experiences of the Mennonites who had been drafted and how those experiences were far from the stated intent of the Selective Service Act. When Edd finished speaking and turned to leave, Haney stood thoughtfully for a moment, then he came around his desk and extended his hand to Edd.

"Mr. Yoder, I didn't think much of you when you first came in here, but after listening to you state your case I find that I respect you," he said, as they shook hands. "I will see what I can do to address these matters."

CHAPTER 35: Influenza and Armistice

IN THE LITTLE TOWN OF HUBBARD, bad feelings against the Amish–Mennonites continued to run high. After the near hanging, the Yoder family and others avoided Hubbard and drove extra miles to the larger town of Aurora to shop for the duration of the war. Now when Edd traveled to the army camps he waited until evening and then walked across the fields to Chauncey Kropf's farm so that Chauncey could drive him to Portland to catch the train. Zion Church also suspended evening services for the duration of the war out of concern that a mob might attack the church.

That summer the Yoder family spent the early morning hours picking blackcap raspberries on their farm and wild blackberries along Rock Creek. In late afternoon, Edd loaded crates of berries onto the wagon and took them to the cannery in Woodburn, but he always tried to be home before dark. Each crate contained twelve, one-pound boxes of berries, and each of the older children was required to fill one crate. Then they were allowed to go and play.

A favorite children's game was teasing the old ram sheep, then running as fast as they could to jump onto the steeply sloping shed roof and escape the ram's fearsome horns. The shed roof came nearly to the ground and the children could run all the way up to the peak. The ram could take only a few steps onto the roof before it slipped down again. But, having trapped the children, the ram would stand at the bottom of the slope until it's temper quieted enough for it to wander off.

The children also took turns riding to town with Edd, and after the berries were sold that lucky child would be given a nickel to buy penny candy. Taggly liked to buy three jawbreakers and two suckers with her nickel; the treats came grandly wrapped in a small red-and-white-striped paper bag.

On the hottest evenings, the family often ate supper down by the creek, where Alice fried pancakes on a flat iron griddle placed over a campfire. The pancakes were topped with sorghum molasses and crushed blackberries or other summer fruits.

As war continued to cast its long shadow, another enemy was gathering strength and preparing to strike. Some said its genesis was in France, where hogs were raised in proximity to army barracks. Others believed that it originated in China and then traveled to Europe's battlefields via 96,000 Chinese laborers who were sent to work behind British and French lines. Whatever the source, in 1917 a lethal strain of influenza began to sicken and kill European and Asian soldiers and civilians alike.

At first the virus killed the very old, the very young, the weak, and the malnourished. By 1918, however, it had mutated into an even more virulent form that killed healthy people in their prime, whose robust immune systems mounted an overwhelming response to the disease. That immune response is called a *cytokine*

INFLUENZA AND ARMISTICE

storm, and within hours of infection many sufferers drowned as their lungs filled with their own body fluids. Pregnant women were especially hard hit: three-quarters of those infected did not survive, and those who did often lost their babies.

In the United States, the first cases of the deadly influenza appeared in Haskell, Kansas, in January 1918. By March, it had spread to the military camp at Fort Riley, and within days more than five hundred soldiers were stricken. From there, the enemy marched with horrific consequences to all corners of the U.S., even as it was killing people in every country around the world. No one was safe from infection, even in the Arctic, where entire native tribes were wiped out.

In October 1918, Portland put in place a set of rules known as the Influenza Ban, and other Oregon cities and towns followed suit. The ban required most retail businesses to close by three-thirty p.m., with offices required to close by four p.m. All schools, churches, and other public meeting places were closed completely. People were asked to keep at least four feet between themselves and others in public places, and homes that had confirmed cases of influenza were quarantined. Ironically, one of the things that could have greatly reduced flu transmission — wearing facemasks — was not mandated because people argued that the actual route of disease transmission was unknown. However, many people voluntarily wore masks in public. Frightened Portlanders fled the city to stay in the countryside or at the Coast. But there was no escape from the lethal virus.

The Yoder family managed to avoid the deadly disease with one exception: six-year-old Paul was stricken. Edd and Alice were well used to exposure to sick parishioners, especially during typhoid epidemics, when they were called to pray with the dying. Alice immediately quarantined Paul in the back bedroom and she alone tended him, taking all necessary precautions not to infect Edd or the other children. With assistance from her mother, well-known herbalist Delilah Troyer, Alice nursed Paul through the frightening illness, although his recovery took several weeks.

Edd's family in Ohio was not so fortunate: sister Fannie and brother Frank succumbed to the virus. In all, nearly one-third of U.S. citizens became ill with influenza and nearly three-quarters of a million died. Around the world, population was reduced by as much as six percent.

By the fall of 1918 the pandemic had reached its crescendo, and many soldiers on both sides of the battlefields had died from influenza. Nonetheless, Allied victories steadily increased and Armistice was declared on November 11. At last, the war was over. Although cases of influenza continued to appear through the end of the year and into 1919, the disease seemed to lessen in intensity and fewer people died as a result. That was fortunate for the Yoder family because, in December, Alice became pregnant with their fifth child.

The little house in the woods was already bursting at the seams with Edd and Alice's growing family and it was clear that something would soon need to be done. At the Troyers' home, the opposite was true: Amos and Delilah's children were grown and gone, and it was becoming increasingly difficult for them to maintain their farm and large house. Now in their early sixties,

INFLUENZA AND ARMISTICE

it was time for the elder Troyers to retire and move into a *Gros Daudi Haus:* a small "grandfather house" built on the property separate from the main dwelling. In Amish tradition, the older folks typically retired to this smaller home, turning their farm over to the eldest son, who would move his family into the big house and take care of his parents for the remainder of their lives.

In the Troyer family, the six eldest children were all girls. Three boys, interspersed with two more girls, came along after them. The seventh daughter, Mary Ella, had died in infancy, leaving seven girls and three boys. By 1919, all of the Troyer girls were married. Of the boys — Jesse, Ernest, and Dan — only Jesse was married and he was but twenty-five years old. Ern would not marry until 1920, and nineteen-year-old Dan would never marry.

Of all the children, Amos had most favored Alice. Now that Alice was grown and married, she had become a dedicated handmaiden to her husband in his role of minister at Zion. She also was looked up to in her own right for her work in both church and community. Amos often visited Alice when he had a problem or challenge in the church community to work through, and he valued her thoughtful counsel in matters large and small. It was not unusual to see his black buggy, drawn by his faithful horse, Bess, standing outside of the little house in the woods.

Amos also had come to appreciate and respect Edd's dedication to the ministry and admired the young man's herd of fine dairy cattle and his willingness to work hard to support his growing family.

On a spring day in 1919, Amos visited Edd and Alice with a proposition.

"Mother Troyer and I are ready to retire and wish to build a *Gros Daudi Haus* near the main farmhouse this summer," Amos began. "We've talked and prayed about this at some length, and we've decided to offer you the main house for your growing family if you will take over running the farm. We'll continue to take some profit from the farm on shares, of course," he finished.

Edd and Alice were happy to consider the proposition, and after further discussion and working out of details, it was decided: a new little house would be built for the Troyers, and the Yoders would move into the big house by summer's end.

Edd was particularly relieved at the prospect, because the alternatives were to either give up some of his dairy herd or build a new barn plus an addition onto the little house, neither of which he had the money to do. He also needed more summer pasture and more winter fodder for his livestock, as well as more acreage to expand his cash crops.

At last, he thought, the way is opening for me to support my family without working away from home and leaving Allie and the children all alone. At last, maybe I have found a real home here in this valley.

INFLUENZA AND ARMISTICE

PART THREE

Home

*"Home — that blessed word,
which opens to the human heart
the most perfect glimpse of Heaven,
and helps to carry it thither..."*
— LYDIA MARIA CHILD

The big red barn on the Troyer homestead was a landmark in Edd's time and remains so today.

CHAPTER 36: Storyteller

AT THE END OF JULY 1919, the Yoder family left their little house in the woods for much grander circumstances. The big, white, two-storey Troyer farmhouse and outbuildings comprised seventeen rooms and boasted electricity and running water. The first floor of the main house held a bedroom, bathroom, living room, dining room, and large kitchen with a pantry off to one side. Around the exterior were two porches: one in front and one wrapped around the side. Upstairs were six bedrooms plus a porch across the front of the second floor. Joined to the house, an accessory building contained a laundry room, woodshed, and two-room cellar. In addition, a building called the summer kitchen stood nearby, along with an outhouse toilet. The summer kitchen allowed baking and canning to be done away from the main house during hot weather to keep the house cooler inside. A well pump sent water up to a tank raised as high as the second storey, from which water was gravity fed to the house. The farm also included a large orchard of apple, pear, and cherry trees, along with several varieties of grapes.

Amos and Delilah had left many of their plain but lovely old furnishings in the house, taking only the few things they needed to make the five-room *Gros Daudi Haus* comfortable. Edd and

Alice had only to move their wedding bedroom suite, Edd's desk, a couple of armchairs, and the family's meager clothing. Edd brought his cattle, hogs, and sheep up to the new barn, along with a few farming tools, and they were settled. What luxury to spread out into that spacious home and farmyard! What new and fascinating places for the little ones to play! Although there was much to do to take care of the farm, it seemed like a dream come true after the simple and increasingly cramped home in the woods.

August was a busy month, not only because of the move, but also because the family welcomed another son. Sanford Karl was born on the twenty-seventh of August and named after the president of Goshen Mennonite Collage. At the end of August Paul and Charity started school in the one-room schoolhouse at Ninety-One, which served children up to the eighth grade. Paul was now in second grade and Taggly was starting the first. Next to the schoolhouse, a yard pump provided drinking water. At the edge of the schoolyard sat an outhouse featuring a stack of Sears Roebuck catalogs used for toilet paper.

Lois and little Eddy were not yet in school, but Lois was now old enough to begin helping Alice with some of the easier household chores. She especially liked to help in the kitchen, and when Alice baked bread or rolled out dough for pies, Lois always got to make a little loaf or a little pie in a patty pan. If Alice had time, she would let Lois make a little *Milich* (milk) pie, which consisted of rich creamy milk, sugar, flour, and cinnamon in a piecrust. *Milich* pie was special, because it must be mixed in the unbaked crust using one's finger to stir the ingredients so the crust would not be punctured by a fork or spoon.

STORYTELLER

As winter settled in, the big house grew cozy with lamp and firelight, and the livestock were well bedded down in the barn with plenty of hay to see them through the cold months. Indoors, the evenings were filled with the children doing homework or playing games on the floor of the spacious living room, Alice sewing or mending, and Edd reading *The Budget* newspaper or working on a sermon. On many evenings, there was storytelling.

Sometimes Alice would put down her mending and add a few pieces of kindling to the wood cook stove. Then she would take a pan of cream from their own Jersey cows and add chocolate, sugar, and other ingredients to make a big pan of fudge. While the fudge was cooling, the children gathered around the living room heater and begged their father for a story.

"Old Rover, we want to hear about Old Rover," they would clamor, and after some teasing, Edd would begin.

The Rover Stories
"When I was a little boy we had a family dog — a big, red hound named Rover. My mother always fed Rover at the kitchen door and that was the only place he ever ate. One day a neighbor man came to our house and he was very angry.

'Rover came on my land and killed my sheep, and the next time I see him on my property, I'm going to shoot him,' he said.

My father, Ezra, looked calmly at the neighbor man and said, 'Oh no, I don't think that it was Rover.'

The next day the neighbor man came to our house again.

'I shot your dog,' he said.

"No, I don't think you did,' father said. Then he called, 'Here Rover, here Rover,' and Rover came running around the barn.

The neighbor man was shocked.

'Well, I shot a big red dog and I surely thought that it was Rover,' he said.

'Rover is always fed at the kitchen door and he never, ever leaves the farm,' Ezra said.

The neighbor man was upset: he felt bested and he didn't like that. So the next day he put some poisoned meat along the farm road, figuring that Rover would eat it and die. Now Rover sniffed at the poisoned meat but he didn't touch it. But one of my father's pigs got out of the hog pen and ate some of the meat and it killed that pig stone dead."

"More, father, more," the children begged. So Edd told another story and then another.

"The only thing that Rover was afraid of was lightning and thunder; when it stormed, he would hide in the barn. One night it was stormy but very warm. So father opened the bedroom window before he went to bed to get some air. Father always laid his clothes over a chair by the window, and his wallet and pocket watch were in his trouser pockets. Sometime during the night a thief came creeping into the yard, but Rover was hiding in the barn and didn't hear him come. The thief reached in the bedroom window and took the trousers off the chair, ready to steal the billfold and watch, but finally Rover heard him and came a-tearing from the barn. The thief dropped the pants

STORYTELLER

and ran, jumping over the fence to save himself, but not before Rover ripped a chunk of cloth from the man's britches. The next morning father couldn't find his pants. He looked high and low but they were not there. Finally he looked out the window and saw them lying in the muddy yard surrounded by unfamilar footprints. When father picked up his trousers and looked in the pockets, however, his watch and wallet were still there: Rover had chased the thief away before he could steal them."

"Around the countryside were many roving thieves who would steal whenever they saw an opportunity. Another night, a thief came and left a sticky calling card. Our farmhouse had a cellar where we kept things that needed to stay cool, like we use our iceboxes today. In the cellar was a small barrel of sorghum molasses that we put on our breakfast pancakes. One stormy night Rover was in the barn and a thief got into the cellar, aiming to steal some food. He pulled the bung out of the barrel, thinking it might be whisky, but when he found it was molasses he didn't want any. He couldn't see to put the bung back in the dark, so he threw it down and the sorghum all ran out onto the floor. In the morning, when my sister Lyddy went to get a pitcher of molasses for the pancakes, she stepped in that molasses all over the floor."

"We had a neighbor, an old man named Eli, who carved little wooden toys for me — boats and animals and such — and brought them to the house. One day when we all went to town, Eli came to bring me a toy that he had carved. Rover was waiting for him at the gate, and because he knew Eli, he let him into the yard. Eli walked up the path with Rover pacing along beside him, stepped up onto the porch, and knocked on the front door but no one answered. Eli thought that since people seldom locked their houses he would just open the door and leave the toy inside for me to find it. But when he reached up to open the door, Rover grabbed Eli's hand. Rover didn't bite, he simply took Eli by the hand and led him back down the path and out the gate to the road."

On other evenings, Edd would tell about his little rat dog, Silly.

The Silly Stories
"When I was a boy in Ohio, I liked to watch the farmers when they gathered for a foxhunt. In winter, when there wasn't as much work to do, all the farmers came with their horses and their foxhounds to hunt on my father's property. They tied up their hounds and horses and stood in a circle two deep. Someone let the fox out in the circle and the men tried to catch it. When the fox finally got out of the circle, the farmers released the hounds, then jumped on their horses and galloped in pursuit. I was just a little boy and I couldn't see the goings on, so I climbed up into a big tree in the garden to watch until the hounds were released and the hunters galloped away. While I sat in that tree the fox doubled back and ran right by me, but I didn't tell the hunters.

When the hunt was out of sight, I jumped down from the tree, but someone had left a rake lying tines up in the tall grass and the sharp tines went right through my bare foot. I ran into the house and Mother Lydia soaked my foot in hot water and bound it up for me. I cried and cried because it hurt so badly. When my father came home from the foxhunt, he brought a neighbor with him. They saw me crying and asked what happened, and mother told them I had jumped out of the tree and hurt my foot.

Then the neighbor man said, 'I have something I think you would really like.' The man got on his horse and went home. A while later he returned, carrying a small covered basket that he handed to me. When I opened the basket, out popped a comical little black face: it was a puppy! My sobs turned to laughter and I cried, 'Oh isn't she silly?' And Silly became her name."

"Silly was a little rat terrier, and when she grew up my father said: 'The pig barn is full of rats and they are eating up all the pigs' food. We'll take Silly out to help us catch rats.'

My father and I got big clubs and took them and Silly out to the pig barn. My father pulled up a plank in the floor by the corncrib and out swarmed the rats. There were big rats, little rats, fat rats, lean rats, momma rats, daddy rats, and baby rats, even grandma and grandpa rats — all kinds of rats!

While my father and I beat at the rats with our clubs, Silly grabbed rat after rat by the neck and shook them until she broke their necks and killed them. When all the rats were dead, Silly and I were tired! I picked Silly up and climbed up into the haymow to take a nap in the nice soft hay, but Silly wasn't through catching rats for the day. She caught the scent of another rat and burrowed through the hay until she uncovered a nest containing a mother rat and her babies. Silly dived for the nest but the big mother rat was quicker than Silly and bit her on the face near Silly's eye.

Silly yelped with pain, but she shook her head and threw off the momma rat and then she killed every single rat. I quickly carried Silly to my father, who doctored her face, and then I watched over her carefully until the wound healed and Silly was her old self again."

Sometimes when January snow lay deep on the ground, Edd would tell stories of his time homesteading in North Dakota, when the coyote got into his claim shanty to steal the smoked bacon, or the mine shaft caved in, or blizzards roared out of the northwest in spring and buffalo wolves howled in the coulees. Sometimes he told of his days in the lumber camps of Minnesota, when he lay in the pest house sick with smallpox and kind women from the town brought Christmas dinner, or when he worked in the icy winter woods where it was so cold that at lunchtime food froze to the plates. Then the children forgot to eat their fudge and their eyes grew round with wonder and little shivers of excitement ran up their backs.

After a while Alice would say gently, "That's enough for tonight, Edd, it's time for the children to be in bed."

And up the stairs the children would go, to curl up together beneath thick comforters filled with wool from Grandmother Troyer's sheep. A brick chimney from the cook stove came up through the kitchen floor and heated the rooms on either side of it, so the children stayed warm all night as they dreamed of howling winds flinging snow across the Dakota prairies, Old Rover chasing a thief over the fence, and Silly the rat dog catching every single rat that could ever be caught.

CHAPTER 37: Guests at the Table

EVEN A GROWING FAMILY of seven didn't begin to fill the big Troyer farmhouse; at first, several upstairs bedrooms were empty, but they didn't stay that way for long. Edd believed that charity began at home, and he lost no opportunity to share his new blessings with others in the community who were not so fortunate.

In the days before federal government programs such as Social Security and welfare, destitute individuals and older folks no longer able to work had little recourse but to depend on their families for support. For those who had no families, community outreach through churches helped in some cases. The least fortunate ended up in so-called poor farms: over-crowded dormitories funded by county governments and private donations, where abuse and neglect often were the order of the day.

One Sunday after he finished preaching, Edd noticed that old Levi Yoder continued to sit in one of the back pews, so Edd sat down to visit with him for a moment. Levi, sometimes called Old Leffy, had been an ordained minister with the Oak Hill congregation near Eugene, Oregon, and later moved to Zion. Now nearly eighty years old and a widower, Levi was increasingly unable to care for himself. Other than the poor farm, his options were limited.

"Come home with me for dinner, Levi," Edd said, "and we will pray together and see what might work for you."

After dinner, as Old Leffy rested in the spacious living room, Edd talked the situation over with Alice.

"Let's offer him one of the unused bedrooms upstairs," Alice suggested, "until we can find him a better situation."

Edd drove his buggy to where Old Leffy had been staying and retrieved his few belongings — a large metal-bound trunk and a rocking chair — and Leffy stayed with the Yoders for some months until his children were able to provide a home for him.

Another long-term guest at the Yoder's table was known as Stuttering Sim, because his speech was halting and his stutter pronounced. Sim was a Mennonite from Idaho who had fallen on hard times during his sojourn in Oregon. His time with the Yoders was challenging for all concerned, because Sim rarely bathed and never changed his clothes. When his odor became too strong for the family to bear, Edd would buy him a new pair of overalls and Alice would coax Sim into the bathroom to clean up a bit and change into them. Not easily parted from his meager possessions, however, Sim would store the old smelly pair of overalls under his bed. As soon at Sim sat down at the dining room table for his next meal, Edd or Alice would quickly retrieve the encrusted clothing from under Sim's bed and take the overalls out to the burn barrel, never to be seen again.

Thankfully, Sim and his long-suffering overalls eventually traveled back to Idaho, where both of them stayed.

Unexpected company often arrived for Sunday dinner. One such Sunday the children watched eagerly as Alice lifted golden fried chicken from the oven, where it had been keeping warm since breakfast time, and placed the tender pieces on an oval serving platter. One chicken didn't go very far, but it was enough to ensure that each family member got a piece. As Alice was carrying the platter to the table, however, the children heard a car pull into the farmyard. They hurried to the window and saw with dismay that a family with three children had conveniently come to visit at dinnertime.

"There goes the fried chicken," one of the children moaned.

Another time a neighbor man passed away and left a wife and three little boys. Edd told Alice what had happened and asked whether she had any money saved from the housekeeping. Alice had a dollar, so Edd took that and bought a 50-lb sack of flour. Then he took the last smoked ham from the Yoder's pantry and made ready to take the flour and ham to the women and her three children.

"But Edd, what will we feed our own children?" Alice asked.

"God will provide," Edd answered.

Several poor farms had been built around Portland, and Edd sometimes visited them to let the residents know that God and community had not forgotten them. On one such visit to the Multnomah County Poor Farm, Edd discovered an older couple and their son who had been evicted from their home and had nowhere else to go. The son, who was laboring in the fields at the poor farm, hoped to get a job in the local hop fields, but for the moment the family was dependent on the county for support. The woman appeared to be in the early stages of dementia, and

Edd could see that she was not getting the care she needed, so he took the couple home with him and left their son at the poor farm to work for his keep.

The couple settled into one of the upstairs bedrooms and all seemed well until Alice noticed that some plants she had in large pots on the floor at one end of the hallway appeared to be dying. As she bent over to see what the problem might be, she noticed a strong odor of urine coming from several of the pots. A little sleuthing and questioning of the children over several days led to the unwelcome discovery that when the bathroom was engaged, their female guest was using the plant pots for a toilet. The problem was solved when Edd removed the dying plants and placed a chamber pot in the couple's bedroom.

Later that summer the couple's son secured work in the hop fields, and Edd moved the family to a one-room migrant shanty at the edge of the hop farm. Alice and Edd supplied the family with bedding and other necessities. They also went to visit them every Sunday, often taking Charity or Paul along, to ensure that the family was getting enough to eat. Fortunately, the son was able to continue working and support his parents from that time on.

Edd and Alice continued to meld their personalities into a strong team that worked well together in church and community. Edd preached and Alice sang, and together they visited and prayed with anyone in need, whatever time of day or night they were called upon.

Late one night they were called out to pray with the Lester Conrad family, whose baby girl, Myrtle Ruth, was dying. The only relief the little girl seemed to find was when someone cradled her in their arms and walked back and forth. While Edd prayed with the exhausted and distraught parents, Alice walked the floor with the suffering baby until Myrtle Ruth died in her arms.

Another time, when diphtheria swept the community, the Levi Sharp family called for them to pray with their little girl, Eula, who had been stricken with the contagious disease. As always, Edd and Alice went together, despite the fact that they risked not only catching the disease themselves, but also bringing it home to their own children.

Before they came home that night, they called the children on the telephone and asked eight-year-old Charity to set clean clothes for each of them outside the house, along with a jug of hot water and some lye soap so that they could wash their hands and faces. Later, they burned the clothes they had been wearing at the Sharps.

Edd also helped church congregations get started. Most people still traveled by horse and buggy, so it could be difficult to travel more than a mile or two to church in winter. Several families who lived about eleven miles from Zion — the Schultzes, Nofsingers, Millers, and Hamiltons — asked Edd to help them start their own church in an unused building. That group of families became the Bethel Mennonite Church. At that time, Zion had several preachers who took turns preaching for the Bethel congregation. When his turn came, Edd drove his buggy and horses the eleven miles no matter what the weather. In rainy seasons the dirt roads were mud almost up to the axles, and in summer the dust was nearly as thick. The older children often rode along with their father, and after church Edd and the children stayed for dinner with one of the families before making the long drive home.

In June 1921, another baby girl joined the Yoder family. Named after her mother, Alice Marjorie June proved to be a mischievous and independent little mite who in later years insisted on being called Margie. With three school-age children, a four-year-old, a two-year-old still in diapers, and the new baby, Alice needed help. So one of the young women from the Bethel congregation, May Schultz, moved in as hired girl and stayed on until Paul, Charity, and Lois went to school in the fall.

May had helped out several times over the years when Yoder babies were born, and they all loved her sweet, even-tempered personality. The only time she had ever paddled any of them was one day when she was doing laundry. As May was boiling clothes in the big copper wash boiler set atop the wood burning cook stove, Paul, Taggly, and Lois ran outdoors into the warm summer rain and played in a big mud puddle near the house. When May found them, they were mud-covered urchins who not only needed a bath, the clothes they were wearing must be washed, too. But the children forgave May for the spanking once they were clean and dry and each one had a big, soft sugar cookie in hand.

CHAPTER 38: Fire!

THE YEARS ON THE TROYER HOMESTEAD were happy ones. In summer, the children loved to play along Rock Creek or in the hayloft of the big cool barn. Paul industriously started a "lumberyard" and used scrap lumber he found or acquired by barter to build sleds, which he sold to neighbor children for round "silver dollars" cut out of cardboard. Because cardboard was scarce, the play dollars were as valuable to the children as real dollars. The play money could be spent for things cousins or neighbor children had, such as smoked chipped beef from Uncle Joel Fisher's smokehouse, or an unusual "kidney tea" plant found in the woods and put in a pretty pot.

Charity and Paul liked to slip through neighbor Mose Hostetler's cornfields and climb the hill to where an old granny lived in a vine-covered cabin. The old lady sat in a rocking chair on her front porch on summer evenings and smoked a corncob pipe. The pipe fascinated Charity, and she never tired of watching her great-grandmother, Elizabeth Troyer, rock and smoke.

Mother Alice always planted a big vegetable garden, and one of the children's favorite vegetables was salsify, or "oyster plant." The humble root vegetable didn't look like much, but when cooked and added to cream it made a delicious mock oyster soup.

Sometimes on summer nights the family picked blackberries along Rock Creek and added them to bowls of bread and milk for supper. Other times, Edd brought home a block of ice from town and for supper Alice would make a custardy ice cream in the hand-cranked ice cream freezer using their good Jersey cream, sugar, fresh eggs from their chickens, and the wild blackberries.

Edd's herd of Jersey cows continued to thrive and reproduce, his sheep were doing well, the lush Willamette Valley pastures produced plenty of grazing and winter hay, and he had planted several kinds of berries: those, along with fruit from the orchard, were a cash crop.

Edd also continued and expanded his community work, which included fundraising to open a Mission for short-term care of the indigent in the city of Portland. The Portland Mission was scheduled to open just before Christmas on Sunday, December 21, 1922, and Edd was asked to speak at the dedication ceremony. On Sunday afternoon, Ralph Lais brought his motorcar to drive Edd and Alice to Portland. Alice was well bundled against the cold, for she was six months pregnant with what would be their seventh and last child. Edd was concerned about Alice going along but, as always, he wanted her by his side and she wanted to be there. They had little concern about leaving the children because ten-year-old Paul and nine-year-old Charity were quite capable of caring for the little ones, and Grandpa and Grandma Troyer lived right next door.

As the afternoon wore on toward evening, the late-December cold grew sharper. At home, Paul stoked the fire in the living

FIRE!

room stove and the children played games and enjoyed playing house without their parents. When suppertime came Charity said to Paul, "Let's get some food from the kitchen, take it into the living room, and eat at the library table where it's warm."

Paul agreed, and while Charity put together a meal, Paul added more wood to the living room heater. When Charity came back from the kitchen she was chilled, so she stepped behind the heater to get warm.

"Brrr," she complained, "it's so cold. I hope Dad and Mom don't freeze on the way home tonight."

As she spoke, she looked up at the stovepipe, which had a vent around it to let more heat into the upstairs rooms, and saw light above her head. Charity knew that a light had not been left on in the guestroom, which was directly above the living room, because just that morning a light bulb had burned out in the kitchen and Alice had sent Charity upstairs to retrieve the bulb from the guestroom to replace it.

"Paul, quick, we need to go upstairs to see if there's something wrong." Charity told him. "I see a light up where there shouldn't be any!"

The children ran up the stairs and into the guestroom and immediately saw that the ceiling was on fire where the chimney went out through the roof. The stovepipe had come apart and flames were licking along the ceiling paper. Paul and Charity ran downstairs and each filled a bucket with water, but by the time they got back upstairs burning ceiling paper was falling on the carpet, which had caught fire as well. Knowing they could not hope to put the fire out, they remembered what their parents had always told them: "If anything ever happens to the house, grab the children and get out." So they threw the water in their buckets onto the burning carpet and ran back downstairs.

Charity picked up baby Margie and took hold of Eddy's hand. Paul picked up two-year-old Sandy and told Lois to follow them, and out of the house they went. When they were safely outdoors, they ran a little ways down the path toward the church and yelled as loudly as they could:

"Fire, fire, help! The house is on fire!" Some boys sitting outside on the church steps heard the children yelling. They came down the steps and started toward the house; "What's wrong?" they asked.

"Our house is on fire, it's burning inside," Paul told them.

The boys ran back to the church, where Yoder cousins Ruth and Rhoda Fisher were singing a duet, and interrupted the service, crying loudly:

"Edd Yoder's house is on fire!"

The singing stopped immediately and the shocked congregation streamed out of the church to see what was happening. Quickly the men from the church raced to the house to see what they could do, and someone called the Hubbard fire department.

Meanwhile, Aunt Ida Fisher came up to the house to get the children and noticed that little Eddy was missing.

"Where's Eddy?" she asked Charity.

"I don't know," Charity cried, "he came outside with me, but maybe he got scared and ran back into the house."

Ida went into the house and sure enough, Eddy was hiding behind the sofa in the living room. After she got him out, the

FIRE!

men from the church went in and started carrying out furniture and anything else they could salvage, but fire was rapidly taking over the upper floor and they could get nothing out of the upstairs rooms.

"We need to get Edd's desk out," John Berkey called to the other men, and the precious desk with all of Edd's sermons, legal papers, and a few family photos was saved. After most of the furnishings on the first floor had been carried out, Jake Hershberger went back inside for a final look and found the family's little dog hiding in a closet, so the dog was saved.

The house was so big that it took a long time to burn. Nevertheless, by the time the fire department arrived, the house was too far gone to save. The only thing the firemen could do was soak down the outside of the summer kitchen and the grandfather cottage next door to keep them from burning as well. Grandfather and Grandmother Troyer had been inside their house, and they and the children were taken to Aunt Ida and Uncle Joel's house nearby.

Someone had called the Portland Mission to let Edd and Alice know what was happening, but said not to tell Edd until he had finished speaking. As Edd stepped down from the podium, someone took him aside and broke the news. His first words were, "Are the children alright?" It took a while to reassure him that the children were safe, and he and Alice lost no time in getting to the Fisher home to see for themselves. It was a tearful reunion, with all family members in various states of shock and distress, but the fact that no one had been injured was, in the end, all that mattered.

IN THE HOLLOW OF GOD'S HAND

The cold light of a December morning revealed the full extent of the damage. Furnishings such as the library table, several chairs, Edd and Alice's wedding suite from the downstairs bedroom, Edd's desk, and some dishes and utensils had been saved. But the family had lost most of the children's clothing; bedding; upstairs bedroom furniture; the children's Christmas presents, which had been hidden upstairs; many personal items and mementos; and much of the food stored in the kitchen and pantry.

What were the Yoders to do? Their little house in the woods was rented and they could not ask the tenants to move in the middle of winter. It seemed the only solution was to move into the summer kitchen temporarily until they could find a place to rent. The summer kitchen was a good-sized room containing a wood burning cook stove. It also had a large sink with running water, counter tops, and cabinets for food and dishes.

The morning after the fire, the men of Zion church brought donated lumber and built two bedrooms onto one end of the summer kitchen. The four older children slept in one bedroom in two sets of bunk beds built against the walls, and the two youngest slept in the other bedroom with their parents. Community members contributed bedding, food, and as much clothing as could be spared. Charity's winter coat had been saved, but the back of it was scorched, so the ladies of Zion Church made her a new one. In the little summer kitchen shack, the family washed up at the kitchen sink and bathed in a tin washtub on Saturday nights, and the outhouse next to the kitchen was their toilet.

It was a stressful New Year, with Alice in her final months of pregnancy and the family crammed into three small, uninsulated

FIRE!

rooms during the coldest months of winter. Edd did odd jobs during the week and cut firewood for a dollar a cord to buy flour and other staples. The livestock were all well and producing eggs and milk. Somehow the family made it through the long winter months, although not without incident.

One snowy morning Charity had taken the little ones, Eddy and Margie, outdoors to play so that Alice could get her morning work done. After a while, Margie got cold and wanted to go into the house, but as she toddled across the threshold she tripped. As Margie fell, her hands reached out for the nearest tall object, which happened to be the wood burning stove, and both hands were badly burned. Within a few minutes it was clear to Alice that the burns were serious enough to require a doctor's care, so she sent Charity to the barn to tell Edd to hitch the horses to the buggy. The trip to the doctor's office was nightmarish for Edd and Alice, as the toddler screamed and cried with pain the entire way. But by afternoon the three were back home with Margie's hands salved and bandaged.

The challenge then became keeping bandages on the little girl, whose adventurous nature demanded constant entertainment. After turning her back for only a few minutes, Alice looked around one day to see Margie outdoors in the rain with both hands in a mud puddle. That necessitated yet another trip to the doctor for antiseptic wash and clean bandages. But eventually the burns healed, leaving no lasting damage.

On April 8, 1923, Alice gave birth to another baby girl. Named for three of her aunts — Sarah Catherine, Nora Ann, and Grace Elmira — Kathryn Grace Elnora came into the world with no crib to sleep in or clothing to wear: it had all burned up in the fire. So Edd made a bed for her by placing pillows and rolled up blankets on the library table, and Alice made the baby a nightgown and some diapers out of Edd's oldest cotton undershirt.

Now there were nine people in the makeshift cabin, and Edd knew that the situation could not go on much longer. As he and Alice weighed every possible option, including going to live on Edd's land in North Dakota, yet another storm was brewing.

CHAPTER 39: The Barton Bridge Gang and Other Adventures

A FEW WEEKS AFTER BABY KATHRYN was born, Edd set out on the Mennonite conference circuit, traveling by train first to Idaho, then up through Canada, and finally to Kenmare, North Dakota. The trip was dual-purpose: the first objective was to continue and consolidate Mennonite congregation-building across the western states and western Canada; the second objective was to survey his land in North Dakota and see whether it would be worthwhile to move his family there. Leaseholder Archie Kauffman had not been making regular payments on the land due to several years of poor crops, and Edd wanted to see soil and crop conditions for himself.

Edd's arrival in North Dakota in June was a bittersweet homecoming. On the one hand, he was happy to visit with his cousins and walk on his land once more. On the other hand, being on his old stomping grounds brought back memories of a more carefree time — or at least, it seemed so in memory. Certainly there had been hard times in the beginning, but his latter years in Dakota had been more prosperous than any since then. Despite his reassurances to Alice that he would be home soon, Edd drew out his trip for some weeks.

His two-month-long absence was a serious hardship for Edd's

family. Alice was barely recovered from childbirth; there were seven children under age twelve at home; and the cows, horses, and other livestock must be cared for in Edd's absence. All of the children must pitch in to help. Charity and Lois helped with the housework, cooking, and minding the little ones. Paul helped Alice milk the cows that were fresh and feed and water the cows and horses, as well as take care of the garden. Even five-year-old Eddy had the job of taking salt to the horses.

Edd acknowledged the stresses on his family in a letter written from the train just before arriving in Kenmare: "…*you are making a wonderful sacrifice, Alice, in me coming over here and you taking care of our dear family and doing so much work. There are few if any women that would do what you do.*"

From Kenmare, Edd wrote that his eighty acres were planted in rye, but the crop was light and needed rain. He estimated that they might see only fifty to one hundred dollars in crop payment that year. That would not be enough to rent land in Oregon, much less make a move to North Dakota. By the end of June, Edd was back home and facing the challenge of how to support his family, even as his welcome was wearing thin on the Troyer homestead.

Amos Troyer was angry. Although his farm was in better tilth and more prosperous than it had ever been, the home in which he'd raised ten children had burned to the ground and that was a huge loss, both emotionally and economically. Rightly or wrongly, he blamed Edd for that loss. Now his beloved daughter, Alice, was living in a tiny three-room shack with her husband and seven children, and it didn't seem like Edd was coming up with a solution to the problem.

Moreover, Amos's boys were putting pressure on him to let them work the farm. The boys were older now — Ern had been married for two years and Jesse's family was growing — and they felt the farm was their heritage. By subtle hint at first, and soon by more overt comment, Amos let Edd and Alice know that he wanted them to move off the property.

As stress mounted in the family, others became aware of the situation, for few secrets existed in the small community. After some thought, it seemed to neighbor Jake Hershberger that his problem and Edd's might have the same solution.

Jake owned an auto repair garage in Woodburn and traveled there every day to work from his big farm in the country. Taking care of both his farm and his growing business was becoming more than he could handle. If I could find a good steward for my farm, he thought, I could move into town and focus on my business.

Jake was a shrewd businessman, and he had watched as Edd Yoder brought the Troyer farm into full health and vitality. If he could do that with *my* farm, it would only increase in value, he said to himself. So Jake offered to lease his farm to Edd on an annual basis.

It didn't take Edd and Alice long to decide that Jake's offer was an answer to prayer. The Hershberger farm comprised many acres and boasted a comfortable house and a large barn for livestock. Edd knew that he could make a go of farming the place and maybe one day be able to buy it. So the lease was signed, and that fall the Yoders gladly moved out of the cramped summer kitchen shack and into their new home.

Starting over on a new farmstead was a slow process. Although Edd still had his livestock, cash money was needed to get the family through the winter and there were no crops ready to harvest on this new property. Now forty-two years old, it was challenging for Edd to do physically taxing jobs such as those in the sawmill: he needed less-strenuous work. In late November, Edd packed a valise and set out on foot to look for work in Portland.

I've seen a notice for a cook that's wanted for a crew working on repairing the Barton Bridge, he wrote to Alice. *I don't know whether they'll think I'm qualified, but I guess I can burn beans as well as the next man.*

Edd's next letter carried good news: *It seems I'm the new cook for the Barton Bridge Gang,* he wrote. *Now I just have to figure out how to get the job done, ha ha.*

Alice's reaction to the news was not altogether a happy one. It had been a rough year — maybe the roughest of their marriage — and a goodly share of it had been spent taking care of the children and the household without Edd's help. Now, as in years past, she sat alone on December 12, their fourteenth wedding anniversary.

Dearest Edd, she wrote. *Well, you got yourself into it, did you? I'm glad you took the job. I won't feel so uneasy about you all the time. [But] I never thought we'd have to spend our anniversary in this way. It makes me sick. I guess I'm like D—'s little boy: he always taught his children to say, "Praise the Lord," so this little boy was sick and he said, "Praise the Lord, but I'm sick anyhow."*

Nonetheless, Alice was not one to dwell on things she couldn't change, so she quickly rallied into her customary role as helpmate, injecting humor into the situation, as both she and Edd could do so well.

I will send you a few books on cooking, she wrote, *but I can't [seem to] plan a meal at home, so I guess I can't plan one for you. What shall we have now, that's the question: pork and beans and cabbage head and potatoes, coffee, and cornbread, ha ha.*

She did send the cookbooks — her two best ones. A few aprons followed along in another package, both addressed to Edd in c/o Barton Bridge Gang, Rural Route 4, Boring, Oregon, for that simple address got the post where it needed to go.

The next fall, Edd had to leave the farm to work once again. This time he walked and hitchhiked all the way to Hood River, Washington, to orchard country, where he worked in the apple-packing houses. Once again, Alice was left to care for the household and manage their meager finances as best she could. She contributed her share to the family income by selling thirteen gallons of her homemade prune butter to a neighbor, but even with the garden and her canning she struggled to feed seven children. The cows had not yet dropped their calves, so for a time there were no dairy checks from the sale of milk and cream. Neighbor Jake Egli often brought the family a 50-lb bag of his unground wheat, which Alice cooked into a breakfast porridge or ground to make coarse bread flour.

Somehow the family made it through the second winter on the Hershberger farm and slowly, almost imperceptibly, the tide began to turn in their favor.

CHAPTER 40: On the Farm

AFTER A SLOW START, the years on the Hershberger farm were successful ones for Edd. His herd of sleek Jersey cows was the best for miles around, as he had a knack for choosing cows that gave the most and creamiest milk. Edd sometimes joked that Jerseys were so much better than Holsteins, the only reason to keep a Holstein cow was to use its milk to rinse out your buckets after milking the Jerseys.

When money came in from North Dakota land payments, Edd expanded his herd of swine. The hogs thrived under Edd's care and fattened to enormous size on acorns they rooted up from around the farm's oak trees. Unlike other farmers at that time, Edd fed his pregnant sows milk and vitamin supplements so that they would have strong, healthy piglets. He also had a flock of geese and many chickens. His barns and livestock pens were always in good repair, and his pastures became lush and verdant from applications of manure and judicious grazing. Edd's experience on his father's Ohio farm, along with his natural aptitude for animal husbandry, now stood him in good stead.

Although he didn't raise berries on this farm, Edd put in extensive vegetable gardens. Corn, potatoes, onions, turnips, salsify, cabbage, cucumbers, tomatoes, and other produce were plentiful. The property also had apple and other fruit trees. Alice canned dozens of jars of fruit and used it to make pies, jams, and fruit butters. She also dried quantities of fruit on trays in the sun during Oregon's droughty summer months. Alice sometimes made a "dessert soup" from cooked dried pears, prunes, and cherries. She also dried corn kernels on long trays that sat atop the wood burning cook stove; the resulting hard kernels were called parched corn.

Paul, Charity, Lois, and Eddy were all old enough to help their parents with farm chores such as milking and feeding the stock; gathering firewood and keeping the kindling boxes filled; feeding the chickens and gathering eggs; and helping Alice with housework, baking, canning, and caring for the littlest children. Edd was a stern but fair taskmaster: every child had jobs suitable to his or her age, moving up to the next level of responsibility as they grew older. But when their tasks were finished, there was plenty of time for play.

As on the Troyer homestead, summer afternoons were spent along the creek swimming, fishing, picking blackberries and hazelnuts, and playing games with cousins and neighbor children in the shady woodlots. Paul, Charity, and Lois were close enough in age to form a tight family group. The "littles" — Sandy, Margie, and Kate — were usually at home with Alice and typically napped in the afternoons. Eddy fell into a gap between the two groups of children: with five years between him and Paul and with Sandy still a toddler, Eddy often played by himself and became something of a loner in the family.

After the long, busy summer, fall was the season for

ON THE FARM

butchering, smoking meat, and making apple and other fruit butters. To make fruit butters, several families gathered on a Saturday and the women sliced apples, pears, or prunes into a large copper kettle, then added quarts of apple cider. The men hung the kettle over an open fire having a good amount of coals and stirred the mixture constantly, using a wooden paddle that had a seven-foot-long handle. The paddle must have holes in it to help circulate the fruit and juice, and the handle must be long so that the person stirring could stand far back from the heat of the fire.

The men took turns stirring in a smooth, slow motion; they must not pause or the mixture would scorch and the whole batch be ruined. It took experience to know when the fruit butter was thick enough to put in mason jars and seal for winter use; youngsters learned by watching their parents. Some families had no cows and seldom had butter to eat, so the fruit butters were spread on bread, biscuits, and pancakes. Children took sandwiches for school lunch made from two slices of bread, cold biscuit, or leftover breakfast pancakes with fruit butter between the layers.

When the weather was cold enough, it was time to butcher hogs. Edd's hogs were so big, he needed help from several men at butchering time. One or two hogs were butchered at each farm and the men traded work, going from one home to another on butchering day. The strongest of the men was elected to dispatch the hog by hitting it between the eyes with a sledgehammer. When the hog was dead, its throat was slit to let it bleed out. Sometimes the blood was saved to make blood pudding; other times it was drained into a cement trough in the ground and disposed of. The hog's hind feet were skewered between the leg bones and tied together using a rope, which was thrown up over a beam or a tripod, then the men hoisted the hog up until it's head was several feet off the ground.

After dipping the carcass in boiling water to loosen the bristles and scraping the hide clean, the hog's belly was slit open and slowly, slowly, its innards were worked out. Care was taken to avoid breaking the intestines or other organs and tainting the meat. The intestines were emptied, rinsed, and taken into the kitchen, where the women were waiting to clean and scrape them. Alice and her helpers put the intestines on a board and carefully, so as not to make a hole, scraped off all the membrane. Then the intestines were put in salt water to soak and later used as casings for pork sausage.

The men cut up the hog and placed the hams, sides of bacon, hocks, loins, and tongue into salt brine for a period of time. Later, the pieces were rubbed with a preservative mixture and hung in the smokehouse to cure along with the sausage links. Sometimes the women canned sausage patties in glass jars.

Beef cows were butchered in much the same way, but more of the meat was canned or salted rather than smoked, and instead of sausage the women made a type of dried bologna. Beefsteaks were salted in layers in a crock to preserve them. Before the steaks could be eaten they must be washed thoroughly several times to remove most of the salt. Edd always saved the cow's hide, scraping off all the hair before he stretched it on an interior wall of the barn to dry. When the family needed shoelaces, Edd

ON THE FARM

whetted his pocketknife and cut thin strips off the cowhide. If shoes needed to be resoled, Edd purchased hard leather soles in town for ten cents and made the repair using his set of iron shoe lasts. Nothing was ever wasted, and everything was used until it was worn out.

By the third Christmas in their new home, Edd and Alice had enough cash set aside for something more than homemade presents for the children. The children's few toys had been lost in the house fire and there had been no money to replace them. The first priority had been clothing and shoes, but finances were better now and this Christmas there would be something extra. For the boys there were new sleds, and each girl received a new doll that said, "Ma-ma!" when tilted. The dolls' heads, lower arms, and hands were made of a hard material called composition. The rest of the doll was made of cloth stuffed with sawdust or cotton batting. Inside the doll's tummy was a metal voice box that made the "Ma-ma" sound.

The children were excited when they opened their presents and six-year-old Sandy was especially fascinated by the Mama dolls.

Mama dolls had an internal voice box that made a "Ma-ma" sound when the doll was turned sideways.

"What makes them talk?" he kept asking, and no one could tell him exactly. It seemed like magic. A few days after Christmas, Sandy could no longer contain his curiosity. He waited until Sunday afternoon when Edd and Alice were away visiting, the two little girls were napping, and the other children were occupied with visiting cousins. Then he took the four little Mama dolls out to the woodshed and used the hatchet to chop their heads off, one! two! three! four! Once the dolls were headless, Sandy was able to dig out their voice boxes and satisfy his curiosity.

Before long the girls discovered their headless dolls and crying and wailing commenced. The little girls, Margie and Kate, were inconsolable and even the big girls, Charity and Lois, were tearful.

"Why did you have to behead all four?" Lois asked Sandy. "Couldn't you just open one and see what was inside it?"

"Well it wouldn't have been fair to just do one," Sandy said. "And anyway, how did I know they were all the same?"

Edd's eyes were twinkling but his voice was stern when he said, "You'll have to apologize to your sisters, son, and you'll be punished for ruining their toys. I think maybe you won't be able to use that new sled this winter after all."

As the summer of 1926 drew to a close, it was Alice's turn to leave home for an adventure. Pickers were needed for a bumper cranberry harvest on the coast of Washington state, so Alice took Lois and Paul with her to work in the cranberry bogs. The work was hard and the hours long, but all three enjoyed the change of scenery. A month spent in the cool coastal climate was a welcome relief from August dog days in the Willamette Valley. Thirteen-

ON THE FARM

year-old Charity stayed home to mind the younger children and keep house for her father. Meals were somewhat hit or miss, however, since neither Charity nor Edd were the best of cooks.

I got supper and we had oyster [salsify] soup, Charity wrote her mother, *and last night we had clam soup, but I didn't know how to make it and Papa didn't either; we didn't know whether to put the clams in when the milk boils or not. Papa said, "Dump them in and we'll eat it." And believe me, we eat every bit of it.*

Under Edd's care the Hershberger farm grew increasingly prosperous over the years, and people in the community began to look at it with covetous eyes. The rural mail carrier, Earl Palmer, had been watching each improvement with interest, often driving slowly along the road past the farm to survey the pastures, outbuildings, and superior livestock.

Toward the end of 1926, Palmer's son was to be married and wanted a place to farm. Palmer approached Jake Hershberger and offered to buy the farm for a good cash price, and Hershberger agreed. The lease was coming up for renewal and Jake was ready to sell. He knew that Edd didn't have the money to buy the place, so there was no point in suggesting it. When Edd visited Jake just before Christmas to renew his lease, Jake dropped a bombshell: the farm had been sold and the Yoders would have to move by the tenth of February.

CHAPTER 41: Starting Over — Again

EDD COULD EASILY HAVE SUCCUMBED to despair. After several good years on the Troyer homestead, the family home burned to the ground and his father-in-law asked the Yoders to leave the farm. They had started over on the Hershberger farm, done well, and were beginning to feel almost prosperous, only to discover the farm had been sold out from under them and they must move again. No sooner did Edd get ahead than he would be visited with a new and more severe trial. At forty-five years old, Edd wondered whether he would ever have a home that would not be taken from him by whim or misadventure.

In addition to supporting his wife and seven children, Edd had the weighty responsibility and constant demands of taking care of his church family: hours spent studying and preparing sermons; responding to calls for prayer and support that came at all hours of the day and night; officiating at weddings, funerals, and baptisms; and traveling to attend church conferences.

If Edd and Alice had not been such a strong team, he might well have foundered beneath the weight on his shoulders. But the Yoder's marriage and faith in God were strong, and together they began to look for a solution to this new challenge.

Once again, Edd considered moving the family to North

Dakota, and once again the news from the Kauffmans was not promising: crops were poor and making a living from that hard land was increasingly difficult. Again, they considered moving back to their fifteen acres near Zion church and for a time that seemed to be the best option. Their tenant, Pete Esch, had been stricken with cancer, but perhaps they could find someone to care for him elsewhere. When Alice told her father of their plan, however, Amos refused to hear of it.

"The community looks up to you, Edd," Amos told him. "You can't just turn a sick parishioner out of your house because you need it back. You'll have to think of something else."

In the New Year, Edd heard about a Mennonite woman, Lydia Ott, who wanted to sell a nine-acre farm near Ninety-One School and was willing to carry a contract. The property was close to the church and school, and because it was right on the road Edd thought it would have good resale value. The farm included a house and barn, but there would not be enough pasture or fodder for all of Edd's livestock. With only a month to go before they must vacate the Hershberger farm Edd and Alice made a hard decision: they would have an auction and sell all their livestock except the horses and two cows in order to make the first payment on the Ott farm.

Alice decided to set up a lunch stand at the sale to earn extra money. With help from the older girls, her sisters, and others in the community, Alice was able to make and sell fifty pies, thirteen half-moon pies, eighty tarts, four gallons of baked beans, three gallons of salad, and five gallons of soup. In addition, she sold sixty pounds of wieners and one hundred and fifty chicken

STARTING OVER — AGAIN

sandwiches. She also sold two hundred bars of boughten candy, plus a large quantity of homemade candy, nuts, and coffee.

The daylong sale took place on February 3, 1927, attracting a large crowd and garnering enough money for a down payment on the new farm. On February 4, the Yoders moved to the farm at Ninety-One.

Starting over again was painful and in some ways much more difficult financially without the livestock. Although they had milk for the family, there would be no more money coming in from selling milk and cream to the dairy. Edd planted several acres of watermelons and rhubarb for a cash crop, along with the usual vegetables. He also planted berries, including two new berries developed in California: the youngberry and the boysenberry — a hybrid between blackberries, raspberries, and loganberries. The boysenberry was named after its creator, Rudolf Boysen, and was later famously marketed by Knott's Berry Farm. Edd liked to read agricultural bulletins and new berries always caught his eye. Berries grew well in the Willamette Valley's mild climate, and over time the boysenberry became a popular cash crop in the Valley.

Edd frugally extended his berry patches by buying only a few plants and then starting new plants by rooting the tips of the vines until he gradually created a large patch. When he had enough plants for his own use, Edd sold extra young plants in spring. One of the children's jobs was "tipping" the ends of the vines to make new starts.

In September, Pete Esch passed away, and the little house in the woods was empty once again. The family was now settled on the Ninety-One farm, so when Harry West approached Edd about buying the little house he and Alice agreed to let it go. It was too small for their family now, anyway, and it was getting to be too much work for Edd to keep up the pastures and the four acres of berries that were planted there. The money from the sale of the little house could be used to make payments on their current farm.

Paul and Charity were both in high school in the fall of '27 — Paul in his second year and Charity starting her first — and the location of their new home was handy for the children to catch a ride to school with neighbors. Most Mennonite children only went to school as far as the eighth grade, but Edd had always hungered for more education himself, so he encouraged his children to continue on to high school. He even paid a small fee to the neighbors for their transportation. Men in the Zion congregation sometimes asked Edd why his children weren't out working to bring in more income for the family.

"I don't see how you can let your children go to high school," Chauncy Kropf said to him one day.

"Well, I can't give them a lot of money to start them out in life, but I can give them an education," Edd said. He believed that education would be more important in the future than it was in those times, and his vision proved correct.

Increasingly, automobiles were taking the place of horse-drawn conveyances in rural Oregon, although horses were still used on farms for cultivating and planting. Edd had kept his farm

STARTING OVER — AGAIN

horses, Doc and Nell, which also pulled the family's wagon and buggy. When Jake Hershberger offered to give Edd an old truck, however, he accepted gratefully. The Ford truck, sometimes called a "cheesebox" because of the boxy shape of its hood, would turn out to be a blessing when Alice and the older children began to work outside the home to supplement the family income.

Alice wanted to learn to drive, so on a weekday when there was little traffic on the road, she got behind the wheel while Edd stood beside the truck and explained how the gears and clutch worked. Charity wanted to watch, too, so she sat beside her mother on the passenger seat.

Alice started the truck, put it in gear, and slowly let out the clutch as the car began to roll down the road. Unfortunately, Edd had forgotten to show her how to use the brake. When another car came toward her on the road, Alice simply steered the car off the macadam and down into the pasture and — crunch! crunch! — into the pasture fence. That stopped the truck all right, but wasn't too good for the fence. Her first attempt notwithstanding, Alice soon became an excellent driver and the automobile became part of family life.

In fall, Edd went off the farm to work once again. Now that he had some experience cooking for the Barton Bridge Gang, he was able to get a job cooking for the sawmill crews, which allowed him to go home on Saturday nights and to preach on Sundays. That work lasted several winters and provided a steady source of income that helped make up for the loss of the livestock.

However, the fall of 1929 brought an event that was to usher in harder times than the Yoder family had ever known. On

October 29 the stock market crashed, wiping out thousands of investors large and small and ushering in a twelve-year economic Depression that proved to be the deepest and longest-lasting financial downturn in history to that point.

CHAPTER 42: Hard Times and Farewells

WHEN PAUL GRADUATED from high school in spring 1929, he made a pact with Charity and Lois. The three older children wanted to attend the Mennonite College at Goshen, Indiana, and all three realized that they could not expect financial help from their parents. So they agreed to work full-time after graduating high school until fall of 1935, then they would start college together. In that way they could share resources and help each other through their years in Indiana.

It was a grand plan, and Edd encouraged them in it. None of them could foresee that employment would plummet to twenty-five percent nationwide over the next few years, or that grown men would be riding the rails looking for work or selling apples and men's ties on street corners. Farm incomes had steadily dropped during the 1920s as agricultural prices declined, but the family was used to living frugally and the children believed their plan would be successful.

Paul quickly found employment at the Needy Brick and Tile Company and was able to contribute to the household income, as well as save a portion of his earnings for college. Paul intended to follow in his father's footsteps and become a minister. Increasingly, Mennonite congregations were choosing ministers by committee

Paul worked for nearly six years to finance his education at Goshen College and to help his sister as well.

rather than by lot, and some larger congregations were able to pay their ministers. With a college degree, Paul hoped to attain a paid position. The main position open to women graduates was teaching, so that became Lois and Charity's goal.

Now that Alice could drive, she began working at the Woodburn cannery in summertime to supplement the family income. Alice was a hard worker and could peel pears faster than any of the women on the prep line. However, the other women resented her because often she would ask to be excused for an hour or two to go with Edd on church business, such as singing at a funeral. Alice would bring her dressy clothes to work and change in the restroom, then change back again when she returned to work. Alice also was the person most often asked to help wash and lay out the dead in their homes, and frequently she would stay with the family for a while to help in the kitchen or with whatever needed to be done.

One day a jealous co-worker on the processing line challenged Alice to a pear-peeling contest. "Let's see who can peel a bushel of pears the fastest," the woman sneered, thinking that since it was the end of the day, Alice would be tired and surely lose the match.

HARD TIMES AND FAREWELLS

Never one to back down from a challenge, however, Alice quietly agreed and the race began. As the women on the line continued working, they watched surreptitiously as peelings flew from the curved tools of the two contestants. The challenger was no match for Alice, however, and the win went to Mrs. Yoder. In all the years until the cannery was mechanized, her record time was never bested.

Lois worked summers before and after she graduated high school in order to attend Goshen College.

Edd and Alice were worried about their youngest child, Kathryn. Small and thin for her age, Kathryn was not thriving; in fact, she seemed to be wasting away. Alice's mother, Delilah, suggested taking Kathryn to see old Dr. Schoor, who had followed the Troyers west from Missouri to settle in Oregon many years before. Whether Kathryn had failure-to-thrive syndrome, Turner syndrome, or was simply malnourished, is unknown. But after examining her, the doctor diagnosed her condition as "short growth," and his treatment was an unusual one.

First, the doctor took a piece of string, measured Kathryn from head to toe, and cut the string to her height. Next, he tied the ends of the string together to make a circle and passed the circle over her head and down her body to her feet. He then asked her to step over the string and outside the circle. Dr. Schoor may have learned this unorthodox treatment from the "granny" or folk remedies of the Missouri Ozarks but, regardless of origin, the "cure" appeared to work. Kathryn began to develop normally and was able to start first grade with other children her age.

As economic conditions continued to deteriorate across the country, people were going hungry, and theft became increasingly common. Edd began to find watermelons missing from his large market garden patch and knew with certainty that a neighboring family was stealing them. The Yoder's dog, a beautiful collie named Queenie, alerted Edd one night and he'd seen the neighbor boys jump the fence and head for home. He also knew that the family had many children and not much to eat. So Edd loaded a dozen watermelons into the wagon and took them to the family.

A few weeks later, when the Yoders were at church, the neighbor boys came to raid the watermelon patch again and met Queenie as they climbed over the fence. This time they were prepared for the meeting and shot the dog with their twenty-two rifle. When the family drove up to the house after church, they found Queenie lying on the driveway, mortally wounded but not dead. Edd sent the children into the house, where the younger ones wailed and sobbed inconsolably as he carried Queenie to the barn and released her brave spirit.

After Queenie was gone, thefts became even more frequent. One morning when Alice sent one of the girls to the cellar to get a quart of peaches, she discovered that someone had raided the shelves during the night and made off with many jars of canned food.

Another time, Edd discovered that his prize rooster was missing. At first he thought an animal might have carried it off, but when he visited one of his parishioners, he saw his rooster in the man's chicken yard. The man knew Edd had seen the rooster, but nothing was said on either side.

"I figured if he needed that rooster worse than I did, I'd just let him have it," Edd told Alice.

In 1930, Archie Kauffman wrote and asked Edd whether he would be willing to deed the North Dakota land to him in return for payments made thus far. Although Kauffman had often failed to make the annual crop payments, Edd knew that times had been hard and that, even in years when crops were good, prices were so depressed it was nearly impossible to make a living. Edd talked it over with Alice and they agreed they would never go back to Dakota, so there was no point in keeping the property. Edd forgave Archie the remainder of his debt and signed the North Dakota land over to him.

Some part of Edd's heart would always remain on those wide-open prairies, where he had carved out an independent and prosperous life in early adulthood. He had met and fallen in love with Alice in North Dakota, too, and those memories were precious ones, but it was time to put them in the past. All his energy must now be focused on his family in Oregon if they were to survive the deepening spiral of poverty that was sweeping the nation.

Across America, in cities and on farms, families were being evicted from their homes. Shantytowns — named Hoovervilles after the current president — were springing up anywhere there was public land; sometimes even along roadways. Displaced persons erected shelters made from cardboard, wooden packing crates, and discarded metal roofing; often the one-room shacks held a couple and several children. Mills and factories were shutting down, farmers could not afford to hire laborers, and jobs of any kind were increasingly hard to come by. Edd watched closely as social conditions continued to deteriorate, and his concern for his own family grew as his older children approached young adulthood.

In her last year of high school, Charity began keeping company with a young man from the local community. As their relationship grew more serious, the young couple considered marriage. When Charity approached her parents, however, Edd and Alice strongly objected to her change of plans. Although Charity's suitor was a Mennonite, Edd had reservations about the young man's family and his ability to provide for Edd's eldest daughter.

"I believe you should stick to your plan to continue your education and forget this young man," Edd told her. "It looks like you will graduate near the top of your class, so you would do well in college. But if you marry now and began to have children, your husband will have no means to support you in these hard times."

Although Charity was heartbroken, at seventeen she could not go against her parent's wishes. Reluctantly, she again focused her thoughts on working toward a teaching degree. When she graduated high school in the spring, Charity traveled to Portland

HARD TIMES AND FAREWELLS

Charity's dream of a college education never came to fruition; instead, she married and became the mother of five children.

to find employment. Unlike other large cities with greater population diversity, Portland's domestic servants came primarily from the white working class and Charity was fortunate to find a job as nanny and maid to one of the city's wealthy old families. Like Paul, she sent money home to her family and saved the rest for her grand adventure. But for Charity, college was to remain only a dream.

One morning Charity was too sick to work. Her employer found her huddled in bed in severe pain. This was not the first time such a scenario had occurred, but this time her employer insisted that Charity see a doctor and the findings were not good: Charity needed major surgery to correct a female problem. The surgery took place in the spring before she was to start college and the patient spent the summer at home recovering. But when the time came for the three siblings to leave for Indiana, only Paul and Lois boarded the eastbound train: Charity's college money had gone to pay for her operation.

There was nothing to be done about it, so Charity returned to Portland to work and continued to send money home, as well as to support her sister Lois, who she sorely missed. When Lois wrote that she had nothing nice to wear to an event at the college president's home, Charity sent Lois her best blouse, her newest gloves, and a five-dollar bill she had meant to spend on her own winter wardrobe.

For Paul and Lois, the family leave-taking was permanent. Paul graduated Goshen College and, while in Indiana, met and married Flossie Lehman. When Paul returned to Oregon, it would be as the head of his own family. Lois also graduated Goshen, met and married Charles Kreider from Ohio, and lived the rest of her life in that state.

CHAPTER 43: Hunger and Scarlet Fever

For the family left at home, life became a constant battle for money to pay necessary bills and food to fill empty stomachs. Once again, Edd left his loved ones and set out to walk eighteen miles to Oregon City to find work. His shoes were worn out; like many others during that awful time, Edd stuffed cardboard into his shoes to cover the holes. His clothes were worn out as well: his shirt cuffs were frayed and his faded pants had been mended many times. In his pocket, Edd carried a dime to buy his lunch.

The September day was unseasonably hot, so when he came to a little store at New Era, Edd stopped and bought a few crackers and a small piece of cheese.

"Would you mind if I sit on that bench in front of the store in the shade to eat my lunch?" he asked the woman behind the counter.

"No, you move along," the woman said, eying him uneasily. "We don't want bums hanging around here."

So Edd moved along until he came to a shady spot in the road, where he sat on the ground beneath an apple tree to rest. After he ate his crackers and cheese, Edd noticed a few windfall apples on the ground. He hesitated a long time before he picked one up and bit into it. Oh! That apple tasted sweet and juicy and good! As he stood up to resume his long walk, Edd saw a car approaching and recognized it as belonging to someone he knew. Instead of stepping into the road and flagging down a much-needed ride, however, Edd stepped out of sight behind the apple tree.

For the first time since he was a young man at home in Ohio, Edd felt ashamed. He was ashamed of his ragged clothing and run-over shoes. He was ashamed that he was so hungry he was eating a wormy apple he'd picked up off the ground and that didn't belong to him. And he was ashamed of having to walk all those long miles seeking work to feed his hungry family. He waited until the neighbor's car was out of sight before he walked on.

At home, the family ate what they began to call Depression dishes: fried potatoes with tomato gravy, cornmeal mush — both plain and fried, navy bean soup poured over squares of toasted stale bread, and homemade noodles cooked in milk. If there was noodle soup left over from supper, the starch in the noodles thickened the milk overnight; in the morning, Alice fried the mixture in the cast-iron skillet until the noodles were crusty brown and that was breakfast. Sometimes there were eggs to go with the fried potatoes, and occasionally there was enough milk to make cottage cheese.

A 50-lb sack of flour cost one dollar, so bread was a dietary staple; Alice baked twelve loaves at a time. When the bread became stale, Alice dipped it in an egg–milk mixture, fried it like French toast, and then poured milk over it. Because Edd loved dessert, Alice always tried to serve a pie made from fresh

HUNGER AND SCARLET FEVER

or home-canned fruit, a fruit cobbler, or an applesauce cake to finish the evening meal. The applesauce cake was a Depression dish because the simple recipe did not require eggs. Sometimes breakfast was leftover fruit pie. In winter, breakfast might be porridge made from coarsely ground wheat, soaked overnight and cooked until tender. Chauncy Kropf often gave the family a sack of his wheat because he knew they were hungry. For school lunches, the children took sandwiches of homemade bread spread with prune butter.

The youngest child, Kathryn, displays a cabbage larger than herself.

The lack of protein was hard for all of them, but especially for the growing children. Eddy, Margie, and Sandy ate their food hungrily: there never seemed to be quite enough to fill their growling stomachs. But Kathryn grew tired of the bleak menu and fussed over her food. When the cows were fresh, the children were allowed a single glass of milk with supper. If supper was cornmeal mush, Kathryn could never decide whether to drink her milk separately or pour it over her mush as the other children often did. If she put it on her mush, she'd have to drink the remains of the milk from her bowl with bits of cornmeal and it choked her.

Kathryn's place at the table was next to Edd's. Behind the table, stairs led to the second floor: a door closed off the stairs to keep heat on the lower floor in winter. One evening when the family sat down to the usual dinner of fried potatoes with tomato gravy, Kathryn could stand it no longer.

"Fried potatoes and tomato gravy *again?*" she moaned. "I'm so *tired* of that!"

Edd rose from the table, picked Kathryn up, deposited her in the stairwell, and closed the door in her shocked face.

"You will sit on that stair until after supper, Kathryn," he said, "and in future you will eat what is put in front of you without comment."

In the winter of 1933, Margie became ill. Her throat had been sore for several days but she kept going to school. Now, however, she was broken out in a rash. It was the dreaded scarlet fever. Luckily, twelve-year-old Margie had only a mild form of the disease and was soon on the road to recovery. Ten-year-old Kathryn was not so fortunate: scarlet fever quickly overwhelmed her frail body and she became gravely ill. Dr. Pemberton came to the house to examine her and afterward he spoke seriously to Edd and Alice.

"Her fever is high and the crisis could come at any time," Pemberton told them. "If she lives, there may be permanent damage." Before he left, the doctor placed a quarantine sign on the Yoder's front gate.

That night Edd and Alice sat by Kathryn's bedside, praying fervently for her life. Sometime after midnight Kathryn began gasping for breath. Watching his child suffer and die, Edd was

HUNGER AND SCARLET FEVER

suddenly overwhelmed by pain and grief. He had borne so much; how could he bear to lose his child? He rushed to the stairs, flung open the door, and yelled as loudly as he could:

"Wake up! Wake up, children, and come down here! Your sister is dying!"

Marjorie tumbled down the stairs in her nightgown and the two boys came in from where they had been sleeping in a room over the woodshed to avoid exposure to the disease. Unsure of whether they were really awake or in the midst of a nightmare, the children stood around their sister's bed in horror, not only because Kathryn was dying, but also because they had never seen their father in such a state. Edd was on his knees by Kathryn's bed, sobbing and repeatedly calling out to God to save his child. His agony would be forever etched on his children's minds.

Alice told Marjorie to kiss her sister goodbye. After she kissed Kathryn, Margie went into the kitchen where the boys were sitting at the table. The three children sat there in shock, waiting, as the night slowly passed.

As dawn stole into the silent house, Edd came into the kitchen. The crisis has passed, he told the children. There's hope that Kathryn might live.

She did live, and as that hungry winter wore on, Kathryn slowly recovered, but scarlet fever had taken her ability to bear children.

In the New Year, a new president took office in Washington. In his inaugural address, Franklin Delano Roosevelt promised to put government to work for the people and reassured the

During the hard times of the Great Depression, Edward Z. Yoder, Jr. quit high school in his junior year to help support his family.

country that, "the only thing we have to fear is fear itself." A new and more positive mood swept across America as the president immediately began enacting legislation to close insolvent banks and put people back to work.

But debts still must be paid and bill collectors came knocking on the Yoder's door. There were doctor bills from the children's illness, a bill at the feed store, and one at the grocery store. Then, too, Edd had made only a partial mortgage payment. When one collector became especially insistent, Edd walked the man out into the yard and talked with him for a long time.

"I'm doing the best I can," he told the debt collector. "I will keep making small payments right along, even if it's only a few dollars at a time, but that is all I can do."

HUNGER AND SCARLET FEVER

Somehow, he won the concession of a little more time. But that night after the children were in bed, Edd and Alice sat talking at the kitchen table and Edd admitted to her that he didn't know how they would manage. Edd would be fifty-two that year and his physical strength was ebbing. No one wanted to hire a man his age when there were so many younger, stronger men looking for work. He was plagued by severe migraine headaches and bouts of rheumatism; sometimes getting out of bed was almost more than he could do. With only a small acreage to raise cash crops and agricultural prices so depressed, farming options were limited as well.

"Why did that bill collector come to my house to dun me?" Edd said to Alice. "He knows I'm good for the money; I just need a little time."

In his upstairs bedroom, Edward Jr. listened to his parents talking and heard the quiet despair in their voices. When Edd buried his head in his arms and cried, his son heard that, too. At sixteen, Edward had hoped to finish high school, but at the moment schooling didn't seem all that important. In the morning, Edward told his parents that he had decided to leave school and go to work. Although Edd hated to see his son give up his education, it seemed there was nothing else to be done.

Edward was able to get a job in the sawmill and faithfully helped support his parents and younger siblings through the remainder of the 1930s. He never returned to school. In 1940 he married Hattie Perkle and started a family of his own. He worked in the logging and wood products industry the rest his life, first in Oregon and then in Washington state.

Amos P. Troyer was born in Wayne County, Ohio, on December 12, 1856 and died at Hubbard, Oregon, on October 23, 1935. He was the first bishop of Zion Mennonite Church.

CHAPTER 44: A Wedding and Two Funerals

AFTER A LONG ILLNESS, Delilah "Lyle" Troyer died near the end of July 1934. Alice's mother was a homeopathic healer of some renown in the community and also was the driving force behind the Troyers' move to Oregon in the early 1890s. She was a true pioneer, settling in the Willamette Valley with her husband and eight of her eleven children only thirty-four years after Oregon achieved statehood. In addition to her medical skills, Lyle had an artist's eye for color and composition. Over the years she wove hundreds of colorful rugs for friends and neighbors on her handloom, turning the piles of woolen rags people brought her into useful works of art. Lyle's indomitable spirit and creativity lived on in Alice who, like her mother, was an outstanding force for good in the community.

Throughout the decade of the thirties, as the country struggled to pull itself out of the mire of economic depression, Edd and Alice continued their work in the church and their constant availability to anyone who needed them, day or night. Many times German-speaking Mennonites who lived in solitude in the foothills of the Cascade Mountains asked Edd to preach a funeral service or pray with them in times of distress. Those people did not attend church: for whatever reason, they kept to themselves. When they asked, however, Edd never refused to minister to them.

In the same spirit, Alice never refused a request to sing, whether for weddings, funerals, or for those who were unable to leave their homes because of age or illness. Alice, Mabel Conrad, Silas Yoder, and Simon Hostetler formed a quartet whose services were much in demand; so much so, in fact, that Edd sometimes grumbled at how often Alice was called away from home. The quartet also accompanied Edd whenever he officiated at gatherings away from Zion.

As part of his ministry, Edd visited mental hospitals and asylums in Salem and Fairview, as well as the Oregon State Training School, which later became the MacLaren School for Boys: a detention center for young juvenile delinquents. When the superintendents of those institutions had an interesting case they often called Edd to sit in on the review. Through his observations and work with such men, Edd formed opinions about future challenges young people might face. In his sermons and writings, Edd cautioned his parishioners that as more children attended high school, problems with recreational drug use were likely to increase, and parents should be vigilant. Edd was ahead of his time in his understanding of social ills; as a result, he often received negative feedback from people who did not want to think about such things.

In 1935, Edd was asked to officiate at a service closer to home: the wedding of his eldest daughter, Charity. Edd and Alice didn't know much about the man Charity planned to marry, other than that she had met him in Portland, he came from a Mennonite background, and his family appeared to be financially comfortable. Ronald Lee Wolfer was a tall, dark-haired charmer with a ready smile who soon put Charity's parents at ease. This time, however, Charity did not seek parental approval. She was now twenty-two years old and had been working and living on her own for nearly five years. Charity simply told her parents that she was getting married and asked to have the wedding at home.

The bride-to-be sewed her own wedding dress of plain ivory fabric. The form-fitting dress clung to her slender body with its twenty-three-inch waist and flared into a softly draped skirt that touched the toes of her white shoes. The dress had no lace or other adornment and she wore no veil. Alice grouped potted plants into a corner of the living room where the wedding would be held and that was the only decoration.

As the time for the ceremony drew near, the bride dressed in her parent's bedroom but became flustered when she couldn't find the belt that went with her dress. After a frantic but unsuccessful search, Alice retrieved a few scraps of the dress fabric and quickly hand-sewed a new belt.

Siblings Paul and Lois were missing from the small family group that gathered for the nuptials; they were away at college and could not afford a trip home. Edward, Sanford, Marjorie, and Kathryn were in attendance, however, and the girls found the occasion as solemn as a funeral. They had never attended a wedding and the quiet gravity of the occasion left them almost tearful. The only comic note came later. When Edd removed his suit coat that evening, he found the missing belt to Charity's dress threaded through his coat sleeves.

There was no money for an elaborate wedding supper. After the ceremony, Charity and her new husband left by motorcar to return to Portland for a brief honeymoon in a hotel. As the car holding the newlyweds wended its way to Portland, Charity discovered a stunning truth about her new spouse: he had only enough money for a couple of nights at their honeymoon destination. Further, he had no job or prospect of one. The façade of comfortable family home and shiny borrowed motorcar were just that: a façade. Ronald Wolfer was broke. Fortunately, Charity now had numerous contacts among Portland's well-to-do families, since she had worked for several of them and had excellent references. A few calls secured the couple a joint position as nanny and chauffeur, and thus they began their married life.

Now the Yoders must do without the occasional five- or ten-dollar bill that Charity had been able to send home. The family continued to struggle along on what Edd and Edward Jr. could earn and another winter was upon them. Farm produce had been taken to market and the cannery was closed for the year. President Roosevelt had created a program that allowed families with children to receive farm surplus such as pork, fruit, and other commodities free of charge. Many families in the local community took advantage of the program, but Edd refused to take handouts from the government even though his children were hungry. And then a fortuitous accident occurred.

It was Margie and Kate's job to take the family's two cows to the creek in the evening to water them. One of the cows, which they had named Ginny, somehow slipped on a rock in the creek bed and fell, breaking her leg. The children were distraught when they couldn't get Ginny to stand up; one of them stayed with her while the other ran home to get Edd. When he arrived at the creek, Edd realized immediately that Ginny would have to be shot. He was upset with the girls for not paying closer attention to the animals, but there was nothing to be done. Ginny's death seemed like a terrible tragedy, for now the family would have only one cow. The only bright spot was that now they would have meat for the winter. Kathryn felt awful that the cow had died through her own and Margie's negligence, but oh! that beef tasted good!

For a time that winter, Edd worked for a German-speaking man named George Schwabauer cutting cordwood. Schwabauer owned a tract of woodland that included huge, old-growth trees; Edd cut them down and sawed and split them into firewood, for which he was paid one dollar per cord. One day Schwabauer drove by the house, saw Edd out working along the road, and stopped to talk. George was a Republican and he began talking politics. He didn't much like the Roosevelt administration with all its new relief programs. Of course, as a Mennonite, Edd did not vote and could not be seen to identify with one party or another. Still, he had his preferences.

"When Hoover was president we didn't have all these 'alphabet agencies' like the CCC and the WPA and that are running this country into debt," Schwabauer commented.

"I don't know," Edd said, "when Hoover was president I never had a dime in my pocket and now I do."

"Not that a dime'll buy much nowadays," Schwabauer said, shrugging his big shoulders disdainfully.

"Well, at least I have the dime!" Edd replied.

It was true: under the new president and the New Deal, the economy slowly began to improve, people were getting back to work, and hope was returning to America. But another downturn was yet to come and, for many, hope still hung by a thread.

Fifteen months after his wife died, Amos Troyer passed away in October 1935. Although his death was not unexpected, it was a blow to Alice to lose her beloved father so soon after her mother passed. Father and daughter had shared a bond that would be sorely missed, despite the trouble that had come between them when the family home burned. Zion Church, and Edd as one of its pastors, had also lost their first bishop.

Amos's affairs were in some disorder: Delilah's last illness had been costly and Amos had mortgaged his farm to Dr. Schoor in return for her care and money for medicine. Now the farm would have to be sold. Edd went to Dr. Schoor and offered to buy the property, using the equity in his house and land at Ninety-One. Edd believed he could then take out a mortgage to pay Dr. Schoor the remainder of what the Troyer property was worth.

Dr. Schoor agreed to the deal and Edd and Alice were excited by the prospect: moving back to the Troyer homestead would give them the scope to farm on a large scale once again. Unfortunately, word of the impending deal reached Alice's brothers and sisters and they decided they must have the farm. A few days later, Edd received a phone call.

A WEDDING AND TWO FUNERALS

"I'm sorry, Edd, but I've decided to sell the Troyer property to Ernest and Dan and their sisters," Dr. Schoor told him.

Edd Yoder's first words when he preached a Sunday sermon often were, "Thank God for salvation!"

CHAPTER 45: Back to the Homeplace

EDD AND ALICE WERE DISAPPOINTED when they weren't able to buy the Troyer homestead, but at least they were no worse off than before. Surely some other opportunity would come along, Edd thought, and unexpectedly, one did.

A few weeks after the sale fell through Edd received a letter from Dr. Schoor. *The Troyers have not been able to raise the money to buy the farm and have backed out of the deal*, the letter read. *If you are still interested and we can come to an agreement, the farm is yours.*

Edd lost no time in starting negotiations. After an agreement had been reached with Dr. Schoor concerning price and the trade of the Ninety-One home, Edd still needed to borrow money to pay the balance of the Troyer property value. Of the few local men who might have money to loan, Edd decided to approach his brother-in-law, sawmill owner Amos Lais. Amos owned property adjoining the homestead, so he was willing to take the first mortgage on the Troyer farm.

"I don't think Edd will ever be able to pay me back," Lais told a friend, "so I'll just add the farm to the land I own next to it."

Finally, the sale was concluded; after thirteen years of disappointments and lost opportunities, the Yoders returned to the Troyer homestead. Edd was fifty-five years old now and four children remained at home. Edward Jr. worked outside the home much of the time, but Sanford would graduate from high school in the spring and could work on the farm full time. At thirteen and fifteen, Margie and Kathryn were old enough to be a substantial help with summer fruit harvesting and other farm chores. It would take time to build up numbers of livestock once again; nevertheless, the future began to look much brighter.

Housing on the homestead included the five-room grandfather house, where Amos and Delilah had lived, and the three-room summer kitchen shack the Yoders had occupied after the main house burned. The grandfather house included two bedrooms and a living room, dining room, and kitchen. The rooms were large and pleasant. Summer canning and food preservation could still be done in the summer kitchen shack, and the boys could sleep in the bedrooms there as well.

Edd was precise and methodical in his approach to farming, and slowly the farm resumed its former luster. As he had done on other farms, Edd planted or extended existing patches of loganberries, red raspberries, boysenberries, and blackberries. He also planted strawberries and developed a specific method for spacing the plants. Edd constructed a large rakelike device that could be pulled behind one of his horses. The rake had wooden prongs that marked the exact spacing needed for the plants. First the horse pulled the rake one way across the field, then Edd turned the horse perpendicular to the existing lines and drew crossing lines. In that way, he could space each plant exactly the same distance from the others in both directions.

BACK TO THE HOMEPLACE

The homestead's orchards and grape vines were still producing well and the pastures yielded goodly amounts of hay and grain. Unfortunately, agricultural prices remained low toward the latter part of the decade. President Roosevelt began to withdraw funding for his New Deal programs to try and balance the federal budget and, inexorably, the country slid back into economic depression.

One Sunday evening in July, Edd was asked to accompany the Peace in the Valley quartet when it went to sing for Ben Kauffman. The quartet, consisting of Bud Yoder, Homer Rice, Dick Mengershausen, and Earl Kenagy — with brother Kelly Kenagy tagging along for the ride — were all dressed in black suits and ties. The summer heat soon caused the men to lay their jackets aside and unbutton their shirt collars. All except Edd, who kept his jacket on and firmly buttoned up.

"You're going to make us look like bums if you keep that jacket on," Bud kidded him.

"Well I can't help it if I'm the only one here who has a little class," Edd fired back.

"Awe, come on Edd," Earl joked, "give us poor slobs a break."

"No, no, I think I'll just keep this nice coat on," Edd said, a bit nervously.

"Now Edd, be sensible, you're sweating like a pig," Kelly chimed in.

"Let's get that coat off him, boys," Dick shouted, as he and Earl stepped to each side of Edd and began to tug his coat down off his shoulders.

As the coat slipped downward, the two men on either side of Edd abruptly stopped tugging and looked at each other in consternation. The other men peered around the first two to see what was going on and fell silent as well. Edd's shirt was so worn that it was ripped from collar to belt. It was that way when he put it on; he could not afford a new shirt.

Just when people thought their lives could not get much harder, events began to unfold that would cause sweeping changes around the world and bring economic prosperity to many — at a painful cost. In 1938, under Hitler, Germany began to invade surrounding countries: first Austria, then Czechoslovakia, Poland, Denmark, and Norway. Great Britain and France declared war on Germany and the flames of another World War began to burn.

Although President Roosevelt promised that the United States would not get involved in the fighting, the president saw an opportunity to supply armaments to Britain and France. Factories and shipyards began to gear up and change over from peacetime to wartime production on a massive scale, putting men who had been without jobs for a decade back to work. Men were not the only ones to find employment: women also were drawn into wartime production work and as the 1930s became the 1940s, the economy soon began to hum at full-speed once again.

BACK TO THE HOMEPLACE

The Yoder family during the war years:
from left, back row, *Lois, Paul, Sanford, Edward Jr., Charity;*
front row, *Marjorie, Alice, Edd, and Kathryn.*

CHAPTER 46: World at War

ALTHOUGH EDD WAS A SELF-EDUCATED MAN, many of his friends and colleagues over the years were convinced he had a college degree. His command of both spoken and written English and his gifts as an orator went far beyond his formal eighth-grade education. How far he had come from that shy first-grade boy who could speak only German! From his time on the North Dakota prairies through his farming days in Oregon, Edd regularly read local and national newspapers. If he didn't have the money to buy a paper, he would try to find one that had been discarded. He also read agricultural bulletins and was well versed in the latest farming methods and crop information. And from the first days of being chosen for the ministry, he studied texts and scholarly books on Mennonite faith and practice. After he spoke at a Mennonite Conference one year, a fellow speaker asked him which college he had attended.

Although America was not yet fighting in World War II, Edd knew that it could be drawn into the conflict at any time. So he turned his considerable knowledge and experience gained during the first World War toward preparing the young Mennonite men of the community for the probability of a draft. Moreover, Edd subscribed to the *Congressional Record* so that he would be well versed in the latest developments and laws passed by Congress concerning military service.

Then it happened. On December 7, 1941, Japanese planes bombed the U.S. naval base at Pearl Harbor, near Honolulu, Hawaii. Twenty ships were damaged or destroyed along with more than 300 airplanes, and 2,400 American soldiers were killed in the attack. America was at war.

Now the family living room became Edd's office, as young men from all over northwestern Oregon came to ask him for help in filling out their draft deferment or exemption paperwork. During World War I only five classifications existed: now there were three broad areas but twenty-one sub-classifications and Edd knew them all. Thus a third job was added to Edd's farming and preaching responsibilities. An Oregon City attorney, Lawyer Hammond, also sought Edd's counsel on occasion and eventually recommended him as an advisor to the State Draft Board.

Only two children — Sanford and Kathryn — now remained at home. After graduating from high school, Marjorie married Richard Larson and their first child was born in 1940. Edward Jr. had married in 1940 and the couple's first child was born in summer 1941. Both Sandy and Kathryn were eager to attend college, but they would have to wait, work, and save their money to meet that goal. For now, Sandy was needed on the farm, and the farm would be his means of draft deferment.

As the United States war machine shifted into high gear, men and women alike were drawn away from farms to build ships, aircraft, and munitions. Now, in addition, men were being called

WORLD AT WAR

Edd Yoder with his namesake grandchild, Edward Clinton Wolfer.

up for the draft. As a result, farms experienced a crucial labor shortage. A father and son of draft age could both ask for farm deferments if their farm produced a certain number of animal or crop units. Dairy cows provided a standard unit of measurement: there must be eight dairy cows for each male family member seeking deferment, or the equivalent of that cow in numbers of sheep, hogs, or chickens. Edd expanded the farm's livestock to meet the required quota, and Sandy continued to work on the farm with his father through the war years.

Kathryn worked on the farm in summer and helped her mother with late summer and early fall canning and preserving.

In winter, she worked for wages and began to save money for college. Kathryn was home with Edd one day when the family of a soldier came to the door. Edd had one of his increasingly frequent migraine headaches and was sitting in the kitchen with his feet in a tub of hot water when they heard someone knocking. When Kathryn opened the door, she found an older man and woman who appeared distraught.

"We've come to see Edd Yoder, is he at home?" the man asked. "It's about our son; we need someone to conduct a funeral service."

Kathryn ushered the couple into the living room and went to get her father.

"Papa you're too ill," Kathryn said. "Let me ask them to come back later."

"No, no Kathryn, I'll talk with them." Edd was already drying off his feet, sliding them into house slippers, and rolling down his pant legs.

A short conversation determined that the couple's son had been killed in battle and they had planned a memorial service for him that evening, but the officiating minister had been called away on an emergency. Would Edd come and conduct the service? Edd agreed and sent the grateful couple on their way. After the door closed behind them, Kathryn turned to her father in disbelief.

"You *can't*, papa you *can't* conduct that service. For one thing, you are too ill to go out of the house," she said emphatically. "For another, their son was killed in the war: that goes against everything you stand for! *How can you even consider it?*"

WORLD AT WAR

"Well Kathryn, don't you see, it's an opportunity," Edd replied. "I have an opportunity to witness to these people about war."

Slowly and painfully Edd dressed in his suit, and painfully he traveled to the venue and officiated at the memorial, his face so white that Kathryn feared he would collapse. She insisted on going with him and watched over him with deep concern until the service was concluded.

The Troyer–Yoder barn in winter with berry vines, top, *and crates of berries being taken to the cannery,* bottom.

CHAPTER 47: Home

FOR SOME YEARS, Oregon berry prices had been low. Black raspberries, sometimes called black caps, had increasingly fallen out of favor until finally farmers in the Willamette Valley were giving up on planting them. Many pulled out their berry plants in favor of other, more lucrative crops. Edd watched and listened to what the other farmers were doing and made a decision. He hadn't grown black caps since he'd planted them at the first home he owned in Oregon: the little house in the woods by the church. But since they were so out of favor lately, Edd decided he would go against the trend and put in several acres of the luscious fruit.

Edd planted his black caps in late summer. After a mild winter, the following spring weather proved ideal for berries. Warm days and nights and plentiful rains assured a bumper crop. When harvest time came, the vines were loaded with fruit.

Well, at five cents a pound, we'll get our money back out of this crop for sure, Edd thought to himself. When the first load went to market, however, Edd discovered that something had happened to the price. It seemed the U.S. army was buying all the black caps it could get to make dye, and the price had soared to *thirty cents per pound!* That was an unheard-of bounty, and with each new load of black caps the farm profits mounted.

The weather remained nearly perfect that summer and berry season seemed to go on and on. At the end of the harvest, when Edd and Alice sat down to total their profits, they looked at each other with disbelief and said nearly in unison:

"We have enough money to pay off the mortgage on the farm!"

Edd wasted no time in washing up, putting on his suit, and pressing the roll of bills into his pocket.

"I'm going to see Amos Lais right now," he told Alice. "We can't keep this much money in the house." Edd climbed into his old cheesebox truck, now much the worse for wear, and set out to drive to Lais's.

Amos was at home, and he was surprised to see Edd all dressed up on a weekday.

"Well Edd, what can I do for you," he asked, a bit patronizingly.

"Amos, I've come to thank you for trusting me enough to loan me the money to buy the homestead," Edd began. "I so deeply appreciate it and I'll always be grateful to you." Here Edd paused, pulled the roll of bills from his pocket, and laid it on the table: "I've come to pay off the mortgage in full," he finished.

Amos was shocked. In a single second, his hopes of getting the Troyer property for half of what it was worth faded into nothing. How could Edd have come up with so much money? But there it was, sitting on the table.

After Amos had counted the thick roll of bills, he had no choice but to write PAID IN FULL on the mortgage document and hand it to Edd. It was done: the Troyer–Yoder homestead belonged to Edd and Alice free and clear.

HOME

When Edd got home, the family was jubilant. Their prayers had been answered many times over and now it was time to celebrate. Everyone piled into the truck and Edd drove them to a fancy, country-style restaurant in Woodburn famous for its chicken and dumplings. In fact, the restaurant served nothing but chicken: fried, baked, boiled, and fricasseed chicken — all you could eat.

While they were waiting for their dinners, Kathryn decided to play the fancy jukebox that sat at one end of the dining room. After some thought, she put a nickel in the machine and slyly selected a popular wartime song by Sammy Kaye and the Kaydettes called "Daddy."

She twirled back to the table, giving her father a saucy wink as the music began to play:

"Hey Daddy, I want a diamond ring, bracelets, everything,
Daddy: you ought to get the best for me!
Hey Daddy, gee, don't I look swell in sables?
Clothes with Paris labels?
I want a brand-new car, champagne, caviar,
Daddy: you ought to get the best for me!
La-da-da, La-da-da, *dat da-da!*"

"Nowww, Kathryn!" Edd said, laughing. "That's enough of that!"

With perfect timing, the waitress brought out steaming platters of chicken and dumplings and they all dug in to the feast. Dinner was so enjoyable; it seemed the family could not celebrate

Kathryn helped her parents on the farm until she went east to college in 1945.

enough to express their deep joy and satisfaction. When they arrived home, however, Kathryn had yet another idea of how to celebrate.

"Let's have a mortgage burning," she suggested. "Let's just burn that paper right up!"

Edd looked down at the contract with PAID IN FULL written on it and was quiet for a few long moments. So much passed through his mind in those moments. He remembered all the long, lonely years when he had so little in either material goods

HOME

Alice and Edd on the Troyer–Yoder homestead.

or human caring; followed by the years of striving to provide for his family — the meager successes always followed by failures, the hunger and deprivation, the shabby clothing, the shame and despair — and now, at last, his dreams had been realized. Edd was home.

"Nooo, no, I don't think we'll burn this paper," Edd said slowly, a gentle smile on his lips. "I think I'll just keep it around and look at it for a while."

On his trip east to Ohio, Edd stopped in North Dakota for a final look at his prairie homestead.

EPILOGUE

EDD AND ALICE had nine more years on the homestead they loved. In 1945, the war ended and a new era of economic prosperity began. That fall, Kathryn traveled east to Goshen College to realize her own dream of a higher education. She graduated in 1949, married Warren Miller from Ohio, and lived near her sister Lois for much of her married life.

Sanford continued to work on the farm with Edd, but his desire to attend college never died. In 1946, Sandy married Martha Good. After their first child was born they moved into the grandfather house, while Edd and Alice moved into the summer kitchen shack.

Over the next few years Edd's health deteriorated until he was unable to do the heavy work of farming. He also retired from the ministry. Zion Church offered to build a small house for them, but Edd and Alice refused, as they no longer felt able to care for a home of their own.

Early in 1954, Kathryn came to Oregon for a visit and determined that her parents needed more care than they could receive from their other children at that time. She convinced them to move back to Ohio and live with her in a *Gros Daudi* room built onto her home. The Troyer–Yoder homestead would be sold: half of the money would be used to support Edd and Alice; the other half would finance Sanford's education at Goshen College.

In late summer 1954, Edd and Alice took the train to Ohio. On the way, they stopped in North Dakota for a brief visit and Edd stood on his land there one final time. For Edd, the years in Ohio were a return to his roots. He enjoyed the time he had with family and revisited the scenes of his childhood. For Alice, it was a painful parting from her sisters, but she hoped to return to Oregon one day. For Sanford, leaving Oregon to attend college was an answer to prayer. He concluded the sale of the farm to Ivan Kropf, loaded his family into their car, and set out for Indiana.

Edd would return to Oregon only twice. On the first trip, he visited his children and held his two-year-old granddaughter, Nancy Joanne — named for the mother he had loved and lost so long ago — on his knee for the first and last time.

In 1957, Edd made his final trip to Oregon in a redwood casket he had chosen and had shipped to Ohio. He was buried in the churchyard at Zion, where he had served so faithfully. Alice joined him there a year later.

EPILOGUE

"Great is thy faithfulness, O God my Father,
There is no shadow of turning with Thee;
Thou changest not, Thy compassions, they fail not
As Thou hast been, Thou forever wilt be.

Great is Thy faithfulness! Great is Thy faithfulness!
Morning by morning new mercies I see;
All I have needed Thy hand hath provided —
Great is Thy faithfulness, Lord unto me."

— THOMAS O. CHISHOLM

GENEALOGY — EDWARD Z. YODER

EDWARD Z. YODER: born July 6, 1881, in Logan County, Ohio. Died August 31, 1957, at Millersburg, Ohio.

Paternal Grandfather: Daniel C. Yoder, born May 13, 1825 in Huntingdon County, Pennsylvania; died March 20, 1909, in W. Logan County, Ohio.
Dan was a pioneer of Logan County. He purchased a 140-acre farm there from John P. King in 1876.
Paternal Grandmother: Judith Byler, born December 22, 1828; died January 12, 1862, in W. Logan County, Ohio.
Dan and Judith married February 8, 1853. They had two living sons: Ezra B. and David B. The rest of their children died young.

Maternal grandfather: John K. Zook, born January 21, 1820, in Mifflin County, Pennsylvania; died June 17, 1889, age 69 y. 4 m. 21 d.
Maternal grandmother: Veronica (Fannie) King, born July 18, 1824, in Mifflin County, Pennsylvania; died July 24, 1888, in W. Champaign County, Ohio, age 64 y. 6 d.
John and Fannie married on January 15, 1844. They had 13 children.

Father: Ezra B. Yoder, born May 4, 1854 in Logan County, Ohio; died October 13, 1921; age 67 y. 5 m. 9 d. Eldest son of Dan C. and Judith B. United with the Amish Mennonite Church at age 18. Ezra B. and Nancy A. married on June 10, 1877.
Mother: Nancy Anna Zook, born October 9, 1855; died December 17, 1881, age 26 y. 2 m. 8 d. On tombstone: I'll soon be at home in Heaven/For the end of my journey/Now I see/

GENEALOGY — EDWARD Z. YODER

Many dear to my heart/Are waiting and watching/Long for me.
Stepmother: Lydia E. Zook (Nancy's sister), born April 17, 1859; died January 17, 1929, age 70 y. 9 m. Married Ezra B. in 1983.

Sister: Lydia Alice, born October 13, 1877; died January 18, 1948, age 70 y. 3 m. 5 d. Married Charles O. Hartzler on January 9, 1898.

Stepbrothers and stepsisters:
- Frank Harris, born September 4, 1884; died November 20, 1918, age 24 y. 2 m. 16 d.
- Ola Mae, born May 28, 1885; died October 7, 1962, age 77 y. 4 m. 19 d. Married Darius Kanagy on January 17, 1911.
- Daniel C., born April 26, 1886; died September 6, 1967. Married Maude Allgyer, date unknown, then Bell Stoltzfus on March 16, 1938.
- Johny J., born July 1888; died September 9, 1888, age 2 m.
- Pheba Ellen, born November 12, 1891; died January 22, 1912, 20 y. 2 m. 10 d.
- Fannie Pearl, born March 18, 1897; died November 25, 1918, 21 y. 8 m. 7 d.
- Anna Edna, born May 6, 1900; died December 15, 1970, aged 70 y. 7 m. 9 d. Married Paul D. Yoder, November 18, 1925.

GENEALOGY — ALICE PEARL TROYER YODER

ALICE PEARL TROYER YODER: born July 9, 1888, Garden City, Missouri. Died June 8, 1959, at Portland, Oregon.

Paternal Grandfather: Peter Troyer, born March 28, 1826, in W. Holmes County, Ohio; died January 17, 1909.
Paternal Grandmother: Elizabeth King, born December 3, 1831, in W. Lancaster County, Pennsylvania; died March 22, 1919, at Hubbard, Oregon.
Maternal Grandfather: Abraham Yoder, born July 15, 1830, in W. Mifflin County, Pennsylvania; died January 5, 1904.
Maternal Grandmother: Fannie Kurtz, born July 26, 1831, in W. Mifflin County, Pennsylvania; died July 15, 1913, at Hubbard, Oregon. Abraham and Fannie were married January 20, 1853.

Father: Amos Peter Troyer, born December 12, 1856, in Wayne County, Ohio; died October 23, 1935 at Hubbard, Oregon. Ordained Deacon of Fir Grove Mennonite congregation. Ordained Bishop of Zion Mennonite Church on June 22, 1893.
Mother: Delilah (Lyle) Yoder, born March 20, 1857, in Lawrence County, Pennsylvania; died July 27, 1934, at Hubbard, Oregon. Amos and Delilah were married January 1, 1878.

Brothers and sisters:
- Elizabeth Fannie, born December 23, 1879, Garden City, Missouri; died August 27, 1972. Married Daniel D. Hostetler, November 22, 1903.
- Sarah Catharine, born January 5, 1882, Garden City, Missouri; died May 20, 1939. Married Amos J. Lais.

GENEALOGY — ALICE PEARL TROYER YODER

- Nora Ann, born — 30, 1883, Garden City, Missouri; died —. Married Richard Phillips.
- Grace Elmira, born December 23, 1884, Garden City, Missouri; died March 17, 1980. Married John Berkey, March 19, 1905.
- Ida Melinda, born April 13, 1886, Garden City, Missouri; died December 27, 1949. Married Joel S. Fisher, March 28, 1909.
- Jesse Stephen, born August 12, 1890, Garden City, Missouri; died August 25, 1964. Married Mary Esch, January 17, 1915.
- Mary Ella, born February 24, 1893, Hubbard, Oregon; died March 19, 1894.
- Emma Isador, born January 7, 1895, Hubbard, Oregon; died November 19, 1976. Married William Kenagy, June 4, 1913.
- Ernest Jacob, born April 15, 1898, Hubbard, Oregon; died —. Married Jessie Barnes, March 12, 1920.
- Daniel David, born August 10, 1901, Hubbard, Oregon; died January 10, 1946. Unmarried.

BIBLIOGRAPHY

Bender, Harold S. and John Horsch. *Menno Simons' Life and Writings, A Quadricentennial Tribute 1536–1936.* Mennonite Publishing House, Scottdale, PA. 1936.

Bender, Wilbur J. *Nonresistance In Colonial Pennsylvania.* Mennonite Press, Scottdale, PA. 1934.

Bernsohn, Ken. *Cutting Up the North: The History of the Forest Industry In the Northern Interior.* 1981.

Chisholm, Thomas O. "Great Is Thy Faithfulness." Hope Publishing Company, Carol Stream, IL. 1951.

Eberle, Donald. "The Plain Face of the World War One Conscientious Objector." *Journal of Amish and Plain Anabaptist Studies.* 3(2):175–201. 2015.

Gingerich, Hugh F. and Kreider, Rachel W. *Amish and Mennonite Genealogies.* Pequea Publishers, Gordonsville, PA. 2002.

Gingerich, Melvin. *What of Noncombatant Service.* The Peace Problems Committee of the Mennonite Church. Scottdale, PA. 1949.

Hadley, Milton H. *To Fight Or Not To Fight.* The Brethren Publishing House, Elgin, IL. 1937.

Hartzler, J. S. *Mennonites In The World War, or Nonresistance Under Test.* Mennonite Publishing House, Scottdale, PA. 1922.

BIBLIOGRAPHY

Kearney, Lakeshore. *The Hodag, and Other Tales of the Logging Camp.* 1928.

Kenagy, Charles Edward ("Kelly"). *I May Be Wrong But I'm Not Far From It.* CEK Publications, Salem, OR. 2004.

Kenmare Journal, Historical Edition. Kenmare, ND. Thursday, June 6, 1907.

King, Frank A. *Minnesota Logging Railroads.* Golden West Books, San Marino, CA.

Larson, Agnes M. *History of the White Pine Industry In Minnesota.* Arno Press, New York, NY. 1972.

Lee, Art. *History of Bemidji and Lumberjacking.* Videos. Bemidji State University, Bemidji, MN. 1992.

Lind, Hope Kauffman. *Apart & Together: Mennonites in Oregon and Neighboring States 1876–1976.* Herald Press, Scottdale, PA. 1990.

Mock, Melanie Springer. *Writing Peace: The Unheard Voices of Great War Mennonite Objectors.* Pandora Press, Telford, PA. 2003.

Mogren, John. "Kenmare Pioneer Profiles." *The Kenmare News*, Kenmare, ND. 1997.

BIBLIOGRAPHY

Morrow, Patrick D., Ed. *Growing Up In North Dakota*. University Press of America, Washington, DC. 1979.

Oihus, Colleen A. *A History of Coal Mining In North Dakota 1873–1982*. North Dakota Geological Survey. 1983.

Ryan, J.C. *Early Loggers In Minnesota*. Minnesota Timber Producers Association, Duluth, MN.

Scott, Stephen. *The Amish Wedding and Other Special Occasions of the Old Order Communities*. Good Books, Intercourse, PA. 1988.

The Kenmare News, Centennial Edition, 1897–1997. Wednesday, July 2, 1997.

The Oregonian, "Judicial System Will be Subject of Judge Haney." Portland, OR. September 26, 1937.

The Sunday Oregonian, "Bert E. Haney Dies at Home." Portland, OR. September 19, 1943.

Troyer, Hilda. *"Our" John Troyer's 68 Feet Under the Table*. Gridley, IL. #1967

Troyer, Hilda. *Troyer/Treier/Trayer Family Tree Outlined*. (Extensive documentation and narrative of the Troyers' immigration to North America and settlement throughout

BIBLIOGRAPHY

Canada and the United States; separation of Amish–Mennonite sect from Mennonite; further separation into Amish and Mennonite sects.) Gridley, IL. #1967

Vandersluis, Charles. *Once Covered With Pine, A Story of Bemidji and Environs At the Time the Timber Was Removed.* Book I. Beltrami County Historical Society, Bemidji, MN. 1986.

Vandersluis, Charles. *Once Covered With Pine, A Story of Bemidji and Environs.* Book II. Beltrami County Historical Society, Bemidji, MN. 1986.

Vanterpool, Alan. *Silk Trains of North America.* Alberta Pioneer Railway Association, Edmonton, AB, CN. 2010.

Wenger, John Christian. *Glimpses of Mennonite History and Doctrine.* Herald Press, Scottdale, PA. 1949.

Wolfe, Joanne. *Interview: Charity Yoder Wolfer Laib.* Salem, OR. September 2002. Private Collection.

Wolfe, Joanne. *Interview: Charity Yoder Wolfer Laib.* Salem, OR. October 2006. Private Collection.

Wolfe, Joanne. *Interview: Duane Kolbo: Yoder land location.* Kenmare, ND. September 1978. Private Collection.

BIBLIOGRAPHY

Wolfe, Joanne. *Interview: Kathryn Yoder Miller, Charity Yoder Wolfer.* Salem, OR. Summer 1979. Private Collection.

Wolfe, Joanne. *Interview: Kathryn Yoder Miller, Marjorie Yoder Larson, Charity Yoder Wolfer Laib.* Salem, OR. September 2002. Private Collection.

Wolfe, Joanne. *Interview: Paul Emmons Yoder, Kathryn Yoder Miller, Charity Yoder Wolfer.* Salem, OR. Summer 1977. Private Collection.

Wolfe, Joanne. *Interview: Lewis Hoffman: the Brickyard Mine; early Kenmare.* Kenmare, ND. September 1978. Private Collection.

Yoder, Alice. Letters to E.Z. Yoder and others, 1920–1953. Private Collection.

Yoder, E.Z. Letters to Alice Troyer, 1908–1909. Private Collection.

Zielinski, John. *The Amish Across America.* Amish Heritage Publications, Leavenworth, KS. 1997.

ABOUT THE AUTHOR

JOANNE WOLFE'S 40-year career in publishing includes work on newspapers, magazines, and books as a writer, editor, and publisher. She began her career working for local community newspapers, moved to the *Colorado Springs Gazette Telegraph* newspaper, and then began a twenty-year stint in magazine publishing. As an editor at Advanstar Communications, she worked on magazines such as *Pharmaceutical Executive, Pharmaceutical Technology International, Geo Info Systems,* and *Plastics Design Forum.* As a senior editor for Meredith Corporation, she developed and edited new gardening magazines including *Perennials* and the Simply Perfect Garden series. She has been a contributing editor to *Composites Design Technology* and *American Gardener* magazines. As owner of Wolfe Media Resources, Joanne published magazines including *dig! A magazine for Northwest Gardeners, Police K-9 Magazine, BYOU,* and *Wild Garden* magazine; and books including *Handprint, Police K9 Tracking, Police K9 Operations for Patrol and SWAT,* and *K9s In the Courtroom.* Her new imprint, Eaglefeather Press, has published *Left-Lane Driver* and *In the Hollow of God's Hand.* Joanne is a graduate of the University of Oregon School of Journalism.

For more information about Eaglefeather Press, and to purchase this and other books, visit www.eaglefeatherpress.com